Fresh Ideas for
PREACHING, WORSHIP & EVANGELISM

FOR

PREACHING, WORSHIP & EVANGELISM

Christianity Today, Inc.
Carol Stream, Illinois

WORD BOOKS
PUBLISHER
WACO, TEXAS

A DIVISION OF
WORD, INCORPORATED

Edited by Dean Merrill and Marshall Shelley
Designed by Tim Botts

© 1982, 1983, 1984 Christianity Today, Inc.
Published by Christianity Today, Inc.
465 Gundersen Drive, Carol Stream, IL 60188
Printed in the United States of America
ISBN 0-917463-00-5

C O N T E N T S

INTRODUCTION

Welcome to a smorgasbord of fresh ideas for the local church.

This book — and the other three in the series — have been created to give pastors and lay leaders solutions. Few problems in church life are unique; most challenges have cropped up somewhere else — and been conquered. It's only logical, then, to share creative answers with one another. If a solution has already been tried and proven in Gainesville or Rochester, why reinvent it in Ponca City?

Contrary to popular opinion, there *is* innovation and creativity in the churches across the United States and Canada. This book showcases that creativity.

As you read the many short vignettes and the longer features, you'll find some that contain several ideas you can use, others only one. Sometimes a single sentence will trigger a brainstorm with which you can attack a particular problem you're facing. The point is not to swallow these ideas whole but rather to tailor them to your situation, adapting, modifying, and even improving as you go.

Most of the reports here were first published during 1982-83 in a magazine called *Leadership 100*. Similar material from *Leadership* Journal has been added to this collection. While not all ideas may be still in place as described here, and no doubt there have been personnel changes in some churches, we believe the value of the ideas stands intact.

As you read, enjoy the good news that churches are doing some things *right* — and help yourself to the creativity, which has its ultimate source not in any human mind but in God alone.

DEAN MERRILL
Senior Editor, *Leadership*

PREACHING

Making Time for Joel and Jude

Jack Archibald has an extra Bible in his office that doesn't get read much — in fact, he mainly scribbles in it. It's his running log of texts preached at his church, St. Columba Presbyterian in Belleville, Ontario.

"Each week I mark the particular passage with a yellow felt-tip pen," he explains. "I bought an inexpensive Bible soon after I came here solely to mark it up. The result is that, over the course of several years, I can tell at a glance which passages I have expounded and — more importantly — which ones I have neglected."

This past winter from Christmas to Easter, for example, he preached through the Book of Mark. "I had also preached a series from Luke a couple of years ago, and so this time it was useful to look back and see which incidents of Christ's life I had omitted."

Eventually, of course, Archibald will return to preach some of the Bible's most strategic texts a second time at St. Columba, and these he will mark in a contrasting color. But as a general rule he will keep searching the non-yellow sections for sermon potential.

"This is a helpful way to avoid having one's personal 'canon within the Canon,' " he says, "and to preach what Paul called 'the whole counsel of God.' "

"What Shall I Preach Next Sunday?"

After almost 35 years in the ministry, Carlton L. Myers has found that the Holy Spirit can guide his sermon choices a year at a time as well as a week at a time.

This pastor of two Baptist churches in Ashland, Virginia, sets aside a few days each summer to plan the next twelve months of preaching. "On one sheet of paper," he explains, "I list the needs of my people that I want to address: salvation, discipleship, stewardship, missions concern, prayer, family problems, and many others. I also list sermon ideas for holiday and special denominational emphases.

"This helps me take a long view and make sure I'm giving a balanced diet to my listeners. Otherwise I might tend to preach too much on some topics and too little — or not at all — on others.

"On a second sheet of paper, I list the 52 (or 53) Sundays of the year, starting in September. I fill in the holidays, special days, vacations and other times when I'll be away; I add dates for any guest speakers who have already been booked.

"Then I begin plugging in topics from the first sheet. As I sense the Lord's guidance, I may plot out a series of sermons as well as individual topics and passages. The object here is not to see how quickly I can do the job, but how well."

When the second sheet is filled, Myers then makes a file folder for each Sunday and begins collecting material. By the time he's ready to begin work on a particular sermon, the folder has him off to a running start.

"My preaching calendar isn't binding," he adds. "Sometimes I feel led to depart from the plan and go to a different direction. But that doesn't negate the value of the system. I would never go back to the old ordeal of spending hours early in the week wondering what to preach about — and then not having enough time to prepare once I decide."

For further reading on the technique, Myers recommends *Planning a Year's Pulpit Work* by Andrew W. Blackwood (Abingdon, 1942) and *Planning Your Preaching* by J. Winston Pearce (Broadman, 1967).

No Hobby Horses Allowed

Everybody files sermon notes, but not everybody has a scheme for telling at a glance whether a subject has been overpreached.

Bob Kerby, who's been at Rolling Hills Christian Church in Tulsa for 20 years, devised a system about five years ago. "When you preach to the same congregation this long," he says, "you have to be careful not to favor some subjects and neglect others."

What Kerby does is use a different color of paper each year for his notes: 1982, for example, was light green, while 1981 was orange, and 1980 was light blue. "Then I file my notes under about 25 to 30 subjects — baptism, prayer, heaven, etc.

"When I start to prepare a new sermon, I go to the file for the area I have in mind and thumb through, noting the color pattern. If I've already preached on that subject two or three times in the last year, I know to move on to something else.

"This ensures a balanced spiritual diet for the people."

Keeping Study Notes under Control

Sermon preparation usually means stacks of open commentaries, piles of random notes, a hopelessly cluttered desk, and office visitors glancing warily at the chaos.

But Pastor Donnie Whitney of Glenfield Baptist Church in Glen Ellyn, Illinois, has found that a simple sermon study form and a helpful typist can streamline the process, allowing him to be both thorough and tidy — an unusual combination.

PHIL. 2: 5-8	5	6	7	8	
Kittel Vol.3			61		
Lexicon		108			
Interpreter's Bible	47	49	50		
Tyndale Comm. (PHIL)			100		
Keil & Delitzsch Vol.					
Barclay (PHIL.)			36	37	
Lightfoot	212				

His study form (see illustration) is a single sheet of paper, lined both vertically and horizontally. Down the left side he lists the reference works he normally uses, plus space for other individual volumes that might be used for specific texts.

Across the top, he lists the verses of the text he's studying. Then, as he reads his reference books, he underlines useful material and records the page number on the study form.

When he's done, he hands the study sheet and his stack of books to the secretary, who starts with the first verse, turns to the proper pages, and types the underlined material. Each verse's material is put on a separate sheet.

The advantages of this simple method?

● No cluttered desk. Only one book at a time has to be open.

● Notes are typed. They can easily be photocopied, cut out, and added to the sermon notes as needed.

● Only the best material has been gleaned. Notes are not diluted by unnecessary information.

Once Sunday passes, material is easily filed by Bible book, chapter, and verse. Thus a personalized commentary is born. Choice nuggets plus the pastor's own insights combine to create a storehouse of helpful information.

"It's great to have all the usable material on a particular verse organized on one page," says Whitney.

It's also nice to keep the desk reasonably clear.

Preaching from a Stacked Deck

After you've preached on justification by faith, where do you file your notes — under "Justification" or under "Romans"?

The powerful illustration you just ran across on spreading the gospel — does it belong in a folder called "Missions" or "Book of Acts" or "Latin America"?

"It seems like we pastors are always needing to classify things two or three ways," says Tom Lorimer, pastor of the Kempton Church of the Nazarene in Illinois. "Yet we can't afford to make a lot of photocopies for multiple filing."

Lorimer's solution: a punchcard system (available from Indecks, Arlington, VT 05250) that features up to 121 small holes around the four edges of each card. Once the categories are set, an individual card can be "filed" any number of ways simply by notching these holes and leaving the rest intact. When you want the cards on, say, "Church and State," you push a sorting rod through that particular hole and lift up, leaving the needed cards behind.

"The cards are large enough to hold a sermon outline I can preach from," says Lorimer. "So I'm able to file an entire sermon by both subject and Scripture. I also file illustrations, quotes, poems, and other material by the same system.

"One of the nice things about Indecks is that I never have to manually put the cards in any kind of order. The stack is always jumbled, but it doesn't matter; the sorting rod instantly pulls out what I'm looking for."

An Honest Way to Plagiarize

here's a good idea!

Each September, Carl W. Garrett preaches other people's sermons at First Baptist Church, Carthage, Missouri. He's not trying to deceive, however; he calls the series "Sermons I Wish I'd Written."

"My book shelves were lined with volumes of great sermons that really deserved another hearing," he says. "I knew my congregation would enjoy them if I could think of an honest way to preach them."

The annual series became a hit as Garrett recycled material from old-timers (Billy Sunday) as well as Southern Baptist contemporaries (Wade Paris, Wayne DeHoney). "I try to find out as much as I can about the original preparation and the preacher," he says. "This all becomes part of the publicity to the congregation.

"I've been able to deliver some of the sermons almost word for word, having memorized the manuscript," Garrett explains. "Others I've had to adapt to my preaching style."

The result: a fresh change of pace for the pastor and a broadened exposure for the congregation.

Two Heads, One Sermon

Bob Russell and David Kennedy preach in tandem. Not at the same church, but 200 miles apart. For the last three or four years, the two Christian Church ministers have been preaching the same sermon in their respective pulpits. They put their heads together by long-distance telephone twice a week.

The idea began when both men preached in the Louisville, Kentucky, area. Churches there had an annual attendance campaign, and the two would work together to prepare a strong sermon for that one Sunday when many visitors would be present. The idea worked so well that they began using the same text and sharing their homework every week.

When Kennedy moved to Danville, Illinois, both asked their elders if the churches would foot the bills for weekly calls. The sermons were working so well that both churches said yes.

On Tuesdays the discussion focuses on the main thrust of the week's passage. During the next few days, they read different commentaries and consider various illustrations and applications they can make. On Friday they talk about the final sermon as it will be preached on Sunday. Naturally, "in order to do this, you must work with someone who preaches in a style similar to yours," says Russell.

Do most listeners know why the sermons are so rich? Not usually. But Bob Russell tells about an interesting exception: "When we were both here in Louisville, a mother and a son each attended one of the churches. One Sunday they got together for lunch and began talking about the sermons they had heard that morning. They thought it was interesting that both preachers had happened to pick the same text. It was suspicious that they should choose the same outline. But when both of us had told the same joke, they exclaimed, 'What's going on here!' Our secret was out."
Reported by Terry F. Phillips, Sr.

Sermons with a Touch of the Class

Pastors are long accustomed to hearing comments after their sermons, but does the laity have anything to contribute *before* the preaching starts?

For six weeks the upcoming lectionary readings were given to an elective "Sermon Preparation" Sunday school class at Northwood Presbyterian Church in Spokane, Washington. Pastor John Pierce used five printed questions to guide class members as they studied the passage during the week.

● *What is the essential message of this passage? (Put it in one or two sentences.)*

● *Do any other Bible passages come to mind that deal with the same theme or issue that would enhance it? Which ones?*

● *What questions emerge from the passage? What needs clarification? Probing?*

● *If you were writing a sermon on this passage, what would you emphasize? What points would you make?*

● *Can you think of illustrations from life or literature that speak to this theme? Are any contemporary issues raised as a result of your study?*

The class — made up of 45 adults from 20 to 70 years old — began by giving several minutes of feedback on the sermon they'd just heard the hour before.

Then the class split into small groups to discuss their insights and responses on the study form. After 30 minutes, they would regroup to share the best of their comments, questions, and illustrations. A scribe was designated to take notes for the pastor to use later.

"My role in the discussion was to help the group look at the text in more depth," says Pierce. "In some cases this meant dealing with the Greek or Hebrew, textual problems, varying interpretations, significant words, or just facilitating the flow of discussion."

The elective class was so popular that Pierce planned to offer it again the next fall. And the questions people asked helped Pierce better understand congregational interests.

"How do you love your enemies when they're out to get you?" one person asked.

"The idea of reconciliation is great," said another, "but how can you do it in a family situation?"

"I learned to put my sermons in simpler language, with more illustrations," says Pierce. "But the people also gained something: They saw how much effort went into making a sermon. Many times class would end

with people divided over an interpretation or
struggling to find an application, and more than once
people would say, 'I want to see how you put this together next week, Pastor.' And they were there the next
Sunday to find out!"

Trial Run for Sunday

How do you spot the weaknesses of a sermon *before*
you preach it?

John Wesley, it is said, used to read his sermons to
an uneducated servant girl named Mary with the instruction "Each time I use a word or a phrase you do not
fully understand, you are to stop me." This curbed his
learned vocabulary and ensured that the masses of
18th-century England would understand him.

Robert B. Ehlers, pastor of Grace Lutheran Church
in Western Springs, Illinois, does something similar today. "On Friday or Saturday, as I visit shut-ins and
make hospital calls, I ask if they would like to listen to
my sermon for Sunday morning. This way they get
the spiritual food they need, and I get valuable
feedback."

More than once a blank stare or puzzled face has
warned Ehlers of a confusing passage. He then asks,
"Did I say something unclear just now?"

"Well," the elderly listener will respond, "I guess I
didn't know quite what you were driving at."

"Well, what I was trying to communicate was . . ."

And after hearing Ehler's revised version, the shut-
in will say with a smile, "Why don't you just say it that
way?"

The result on Sunday morning is "a greatly im-
proved message," says the pastor. "Sometimes, we
preachers stay locked up in our studies and don't make
good sense. We need the honest reactions of those who
have to listen to us."

PREACHING EFFECTIVELY — WITHOUT NOTES

by Craig Skinner, professor of practical theology,
Talbot Theological Seminary, La Mirada, California

Can you imagine standing in your pulpit with the briefest of notes, or even with none? What would it be like to stand free and open next Sunday morning and fix the congregational eye unlimited and unencumbered by a notes barrier? Would it help release your thoughts and words and propel them into communication unbound by the shackles of paper?

Such an experience casts the preacher into an immediate dialogue with his listeners, stimulating their minds and emotions, as the Holy Spirit uses the full resources of the human personality to communicate God's truth. When communication becomes intimate, direct, and powerful, its content increases in challenge and acceptability. The potential for effective results is immensely multiplied.

It's impossible to imagine the apostle Paul feverishly flipping through sermon notes as he approached Mars' Hill, or Jesus constantly glancing at a scroll in his lap or artfully cupping scraps of parchment in his outstretched hand. One is reminded of a story attributed to Spurgeon, who when asked to comment on a student's sermon said, "Well, only three things were wrong with it. He read it, he read it badly, and it wasn't worth reading."

While Billy Graham obviously possesses unique communicative gifts, he readily admits that his freedom in the pulpit, liberty in articulation, and the power to retain the attention of his audience come through careful discipline and hard work.

Recently, he cited two major concerns: material saturation and commitment to illustrations. For the first five or six years of his ministry he wrote his sermons in full, and often preached each one up to twenty-five times before facing an audience. "I would find an empty church or building," he said, "and preach that sermon until I knew my outline, where my stories fit, and exactly what I was going to say." Even today, despite the verbal skills that have come with maturity, he still writes out a potential sermon word for word. But now, as then, he carries as little paper into the pulpit as possible.

Dynamic preaching combines intellectual and emotional momentum. Revelation plus personal insight builds an escalating strength in the best sermons that demands a freedom only note-free preaching can sustain. Written notes retard those forces just when they ought to crescendo, igniting the fire of congregational response. If the preacher cannot master enough logic and enthusiasm to buoyantly carry himself from introduction to conclusion, how can he reasonably expect those who listen to do so? The good news is that whether you have preached three or thirty years, you can move successfully into effective and enthusiastic extemporaneous delivery.

One quick caution: please note that extemporaneous does not mean impromptu. The latter implies deciding what to say at the time of delivery. The former encompasses a thorough preparation right through to summary notes, but refuses to limit delivery by their use in the pulpit.

How can this happen? Recently, a group of advanced graduate students and I entered into correspondence with Harold L. Adams, pastor of First Baptist Church, Downey, California. He has served thirteen years in his present pastorate and has mastered the art of attractive exposition using only a small Bible while in the pulpit. Adams suggests the following practices.

1. *Structural strength*. A clear outline is the first step to pulpit freedom. Materials arranged in proper sequence always help extemporaneous delivery. The main track of thought from introduction to conclusion with appropriate stops for emphasis of major points allows the journey to be completed on time and with satisfaction. Related sidelines must always be quickly channeled back to the main line. A "logical" memory always provides a better assistance than a "verbal" memory.

2. *Material saturation*. Like Billy Graham, Adams regards a thorough grasp of the material as the major factor in all good preaching, especially extemporaneous preaching. Only when the mind is saturated with the material can preaching come "out of the overflow" rather than from an ever-diminishing trickle. While different preachers follow differing methods, saturation through writing still remains one of the best disciplines for preaching. Ideas have no clarity unless shaped into words and sentences. The average preacher will find little fluency simply by brooding over his outline all week without disciplining himself to write about it. Total invention at the point of delivery is almost impossible for most preachers.

Written expression gives a tangible way of capturing concepts and meditating on them, while the specific words used in the verbal presentation can be left to the inspiration of the delivery moment. Once the material is written, begin preaching it aloud. Many speakers record their message on tape and play it back many times while preaching along with the recording. Writing out a sermon word-for-word and then preaching it aloud many times will guarantee material saturation.

3. *Key sentence memorization*. Word precision reaches an apex in the introduction, conclusion, and at major divisions of the outline. Short, sharp sentences hit hard and stick. Total memorization usually keeps the speaker so busy with recall that he's unable to respond to the communication needs of

the moment. Thus, the logical flow of the sermon should be captured in crisp phrases that become keys to unlocking larger sections of thought or encapsulating them with clarity. The punch line of a proposition is prime material to fix in the memory for recall during delivery.

4. *Mastery of segmented sections.* Adams says, "Very few preachers are brilliant enough to master a thirty-minute essay, but most speakers have the ability to master a five-minute speech." Why not turn a thirty-minute sermon into six five-minute speeches? Work on each section as a distinct unit. These can then be woven together by carefully planned transitions, bridging sentences, and well-placed illustrations. Rehearsed as a whole, the sermon will develop a unified flow that provides the preacher with an ever-growing sense of mastery.

A word about illustrations: Every great preacher has mastered the art of choosing and telling illustrative stories. They are the windows of every sermon; they let the light shine in while allowing the people to see out. Learn the art of good storytelling. It may make the difference between what your people remember and what they forget about your sermon. Jesus seldom spoke without telling a story.

5. *Presentation.* Obviously, extemporaneous delivery ought not be attempted under severe physical or emotional strain. Delivery should be preceded by a period of rest, meditation, and prayer. It is still the practice of Billy Graham to spend several hours of uninterrupted concentration on his material immediately prior to delivery. He recently said, "I spend that time doing three things: I rest because I need to have my physical strength; I pray; and I just think on what I'm going to say, asking the Lord to give me new and fresh thoughts even though I may have preached the sermon before."

If you cannot go into the pulpit without your sermon notes, limit yourself to a single slip of paper that can be put in the pages of your Bible. Force yourself to preach whole sections of your message without looking at your notes. Step back from the pulpit or to one side, turn to the choir behind you, or speak to one section of the congregation with an "abandonment by faith" to direct eye-to-eye delivery.

Of course you will fail sometimes! The human condition is always subject to moods and feelings, and you may not always speak as you desire. Grammatical slips may occur; words may tumble out too fast; but the only way to swim is to launch out and start swimming. Whitefield, Spurgeon, Beecher, and a score of others mastered preaching without notes by employing this kind of discipline, faith, and courage.

A determined commitment to aim for extemporaneous delivery will more than motivate you toward its achievement. I know. After thirty years of preaching with notes as a pastor and professor, I recently tackled a seminary chapel in the above manner. I had never before been totally note-free. This time, I not only abandoned notes but also Bible, pulpit, and lavaliere microphone. Pacing as close to my audience as I could, I preached on a subject I had never before presented. The audience was totally with me for twenty-five minutes. Before anyone could respond, I knew I had effectively communicated in a whole new way.

I probably will not be able to do this in all my speaking assignments, but I certainly intend to try. The results were far above those I ever expected.

Preaching in Spite of a Headache

The best study, prayer, and meditation can go for naught on Sunday morning if the preacher does not put his personal problems aside, says Per W. Larsen, pastor of 59th Street Lutheran Brethren Church in Brooklyn.

"I carry on a little dialogue with myself as I drive to the church each week. I remind myself that God is not interested in having a defeated messenger in the pulpit. He wants his Word to go forth with power and conviction. My own inner problems, family conflicts, or depressive thoughts can wait."

Clinical training was what started Larsen using his 20-minute drive through the city streets — usually at their quietest on early Sunday mornings — to prepare himself psychologically to preach. "I had never thought much about how a sermon can be colored by one's emotional state," he says. "I resolved that I would begin using my drive time to remind myself of God's purposes for the morning and dismiss my private problems until later.

"John Bunyan once said of a low period of his life, 'I walked around in chains and spoke to people in chains, but once in the pulpit my chains fell off.'

"Sometimes I don't sleep well and awaken on Sunday morning with a tension headache. But even then I can make an effort of the will to concentrate on one thing: that the audience receive a message through me. What a release it is to be in control of one's own hang-ups."

Empty Stomach, Full Heart

When Steve Wake preached on hunger relief at First Baptist Church in Cement, Oklahoma, no one could say he didn't know his subject. He had fasted the previous four days.

"When I began sermon preparation back on Monday," the pastor recalls, "I sat down at my desk right after a quick trip to the convenience store. There I was — my open Bible, a can of pop, and a package of peanuts — the irony of it all came flooding in on me. How ridiculous to be munching my way through my message.

"I stopped and spent some honest time praying and thinking. I felt impressed to restrict myself to water only so I could experience hunger personally." He began his fast the next day and did not break it until Saturday evening.

What he learned formed the introduction of his sermon. His text was Christ's prayer "Give us this day our daily bread" from Matthew 6. "I emphasized that many people in the world have to pray such a prayer in earnest, whereas most of us repeat it only casually."

Wake's newfound compassion for the hungry apparently struck a nerve in the congregation. The closing offering for hunger relief, even though unannounced in advance, was greater than any such offering in the church's history.

The Text Comes Alive

Members of St. Paul's United Methodist Church in Defiance, Ohio, have never heard their current pastor read the Bible during a service. Instead, George Holcombe repeats the Scripture verses from memory.

"It started about 15 years ago when I was using a psalm," says Holcombe. "I thought it would sound more like poetry if I spoke it rather than read it. I never went back to reading the Scripture in church."

While Holcombe has recited as many as 22 verses at one time, he tries to keep the Scripture lesson to betweeen 6 and 11 verses. He memorizes by reading the words aloud over and over the week before he uses them. The shorter texts take him only about a half-hour to learn; longer sections take more time, but he has no special tricks for memorizing. He has simply found that the more he does it, the easier it gets.

What if his mind should draw a blank some Sunday? Holcombe has a Bible beside him, and once or twice he has had to open it to get the first word of the next sentence. But then he has continued from memory.

"The hardest part," he says, "is the first word of a new sentence. After you have the first word, it's not hard to go on."

The chief advantage to quoting, of course, is the constant eye contact with the listeners. "When he says the verses," one member comments, "it makes it seem like it happened yesterday and not thousands of years ago."

Reported by Betty Steele Everett

Pastor Jim Carpenter of Fellowship Baptist Church in Chino, California, doesn't attempt to memorize his texts, but he, like Holcombe, believes in saturating his week with the spoken Word.

"At the beginning of my sermon preparation," he says, "I sit down with a cassette machine and record my text from as many different versions as I can find — usually six or seven. I also record the verses in the original language and supply my own translation.

"Then, as I drive on hospital calls and other trips, I permeate my mind with this passage of Scripture. I end up listening to the text dozens of times, and when I get back to my desk to prepare my message, I'm very familiar with the theme and flow of thought.

"It's a good way to redeem my travel time for the specific benefit of next Sunday morning's sermon."

Harnessing Doodle Power

Every preacher knows the deflated feeling that comes when listeners lose their concentration, gaze vacantly into space, or doodle on the bulletin.

Kelvin Mutter, pastor of Milton Baptist Church in Ontario, decided to make doodling work *for* him, not against him.

"One method I've found effective is to encourage people to draw a diagram of the word picture being described in the sermon text," he says.

In a recent sermon on Romans 11, for instance, he suggested everyone draw two trees side by side — one well-groomed and the other wild.

"After discussing how the two trees are like people separated from God and those who are his people, I asked them to erase one branch from the wild tree and redraw it on the groomed tree. At that point, I explained the process of grafting and what it means for us to be grafted into Christ."

Mutter points out other passages that lend themselves to self-illustrating doodles: Isaiah 11, Daniel 5, Amos 7, and John 15.

"The impact of messages delivered this way is heightened," says Mutter, "because listeners use their ears, eyes, hands, and imagination to follow the sermon."

Where the Crowd Talks Back

Preachers have raised rhetorical questions forever, but in at least one Los Angeles church, the speaker sometimes gets answers from the pews.

William Pile, pastor of Highland Park Church of Christ, recently planted six members in the audience to call out responses during a sermon on Cornelius entitled "A Good Man Made Better." When Pile came to the point of asking, "What is your claim to moral goodness?" the first man piped up, "Well, I've never killed anybody."

The second said, "I say my prayers every night."

Then, "I give blood to the Red Cross regularly."

"I came from a fine Christian family."

Everyone was wide-awake by then — and to the preacher's surprise, some began jumping in spontaneously. One woman said, "I always help people — at least the ones I like!" which illustrated the sermon's thrust perfectly. No one could escape the point that claims to religious devotion are no substitute for knowing Christ.

"I've used the technique three or four times since then," Pile reports, "sometimes even to argue or take exception with something I've said. Naturally, I keep it infrequent enough to retain the surprise factor. But I can tell you, people don't do much dozing during the sermons these days. Especially the 'plants' — they might miss my cue."

One Answer to the Summer Slump

Preaching during the summer months can be discouraging, when even the most regular members are sporadic in attendance. Sermon series lose their continuity, and while topical preaching is fine, pastors often feel the "people who needed that one" were out sailing that weekend.

"About five years ago I tried a new approach," says Harvey D. Moore of First Christian Church (Disciples of Christ) in Liberal, Kansas. "I announced in September that the following summer we would have a three-month series on problem passages of Scripture. The congregation was asked to jot down any passage or doctrine they found difficult to understand. I would put them all in a sequence for the summer sermons."

Questions flowed naturally out of Sunday school classes, books being read, TV debates, and other situations. An occasional reminder was published in the church newsletter, and by December, Moore had enough requests to fill the 13 Sundays.

He then published the summer preaching schedule and encouraged people to research the topics in advance. "The results have been amazing," he says.

"1. The congregation feels their questions are being taken seriously.

"2. People have begun to do fairly serious reading about difficult texts and wrestle with the implication of most of the doctrines.

"3. It has forced me to dig and study in some areas I needed to look at more thoroughly.

"4. In most cases, folks make it a point to be in church the day their question is being discussed.

"5. In some instances, impromptu gatherings for lunch have taken place to finish the discussion; thus, fellowship is enhanced.

"In all, it's been successful and has become one of the high points of the preaching year."

Keeping a Sermon Series Alive

Thirty years ago, the people who heard Pastor Carlton Myers preach a series got tired of listening to sermons from the same Bible book for several months.

Today, Myers still preaches series in his two Baptist churches in Ashland, Virginia — but only about one sermon a month.

"The sermons are then close enough that the congregation doesn't forget the previous ones," he says, "but far enough apart so as not to be boring or tiring."

Preaching through the Book of Philippians on four consecutive Sundays may be manageable, but a series on Hebrews or Mark or the doctrine of the church can seem to go on forever. By spreading it out with installments every third or fourth week, the continuity is retained while the intervening Sundays provide variety. "You may not mine all the gold," Myers observes, "but what you do mine is more likely to be cherished by the listeners."

A Bible Series: Tying It All Together

When First Congregational Church of Emerald Grove, Wisconsin, listened to their pastor preach though the books of the Bible, they wound up with something to show for it. Together they created a queen-sized quilt with a square for each of the 66 books. It now hangs on a side wall of the sanctuary.

"We began our emphasis on 'The Holy Bible . . . Textbook for Life' on the first Sunday of Lent, 1981," says Pastor John Eyster. "I finished up on Reformation Sunday, 1982, with a great celebration." (Eyster departed from his series occasionally for holidays, vacations times, and also did several summary sermons, so that the entire series took 20 months.)

Meanwhile, Vicki Duoss, a member of the congregation who manages a local fabric shop and teaches classes on quilting, was coordinating the Bible hanging.

"We tried to get one square from each family in the church," says the pastor, "and came very close to our goal. More than just the women participated; one square was designed and sewn by a 12-year-old boy."

Duoss prepared an instruction sheet to guide the volunteers, and also assembled the pieces in the end. At the unveiling, oohs and ahhs greeted the colorful collage. "People were happily surprised with how creative everyone had been," Eyster reports. "They gathered round to study it and try to identify the various books." Jonah's fish and Daniel's den of lions weren't hard, but others were more symbolic. An index was available to help.

"Since then we've had visitors come to the church just to see the hanging," says the pastor. "It has generated a great deal of interest."

A Book in the Hand Beats 66 on the Shelf

A sermon series on a book of the Bible often has two strikes against it: (1) not everyone brings a Bible in order to follow the preaching, and (2) those who do bring varying translations.

Throughout his ministry, Luther Cross has solved both problems by handing out an American Bible Society pocket edition of the book on the series' first Sunday. Most recently at Center Presbyterian Church in Seaton, Illinois, his treatments of Philippians, 1 Corinthians, and other books were enriched by every listener holding a handy copy of the text.

ABS editions are inexpensive (25¢ or less), available in King James, Revised Standard, and Good News versions, and cover the entire New Testament plus Psalms and Proverbs.

"We also provided mimeographed outlines of the Bible book," says Cross, who now works full-time in Bible translation. "I tried to involved laymen as frequently as possible through reflections and plays that related to the text.

"But the handout booklets were the most strategic. Everyone had the same text in a form small enough for a shirt pocket or purse. They could use it not only in church but take it along to read any time."

You Don't Say . . . Someone Else Does

33

Donahue does it. Carson does it. Even Pat Robertson does it . . . and with excellent results. Dialogue — a simple conversation with an interesting person — can be educational, entertaining, and for Christians, even edifying. But in church?

"I'd read about dialogue sermons, of course, but they sounded so stilted," says Tom Wadsworth, minister at Dixon (Illinois) Church of Christ. "I'd never actually seen it done, and I never had the courage to try it."

A weekend house guest, however, gave Wadsworth the chance to experiment.

"This particular friend was 25 years old and had struggled, successfully, with a drinking and a drug abuse problem. I felt a dialogue with someone who had 'been there' might be more effective than a typical sermon approach in persuading young people to stop their alcohol and marijuana habits," says Wadsworth.

Using an interview format, Wadsworth stood at the pulpit asking prepared questions, and his friend, standing nearby at a lectern, gave candid responses. Only Wadsworth had notes so the responses could be spontaneous and natural. If his friend forgot to mention certain planned points or appropriate Scripture, the minister could probe that area to spark his memory. He also broadened the dialogue to include the general problem of struggles and depression in order to make it apply to everyone.

"During the dialogue, I couldn't bring myself to look at the congregation for fear that it wasn't going over," Wadsworth admits. But to his surprise, the people were enthusiastic.

Four Ways to Open the Pulpit to Laity

A roundup of ideas from the East, South, and Midwest:

The diaconate board of Drexel Hill (Pa.) Baptist Church came up with the idea of having a Mother's Day speaker who had actually experienced motherhood. They ended up selecting three women of the church to collaborate on a three-point outline the pastor and board created. Each was allotted five to eight minutes.

A mother of three school-age children spoke on "Mothers Called," a mother of two toddlers spoke on "Mothers Equipped," and a grandmother spoke on "A Mother's Legacy." Few dry eyes could be found in the church.

Observation: One third of a sermon is more manageable for a lay speaker than the whole thing.
Reported by Marlene Bagnull

Pastor Robert J. Berry has a promising young man in the Fountain Lake United Methodist Church, Hot Springs, Arkansas. "I've assigned him to preach the fifth Sundays thoughout the year.

"This gives him a fixed date well in advance and spreads his opportunities neatly. I like it, and he has re-sponded very positively."

Fifth Sundays are special at Faith Covenant Church in Wheaton, Illinois, too, for a variety of reasons. On those mornings, Pastor John Benson sits in the con-gregation with his family while the worship committee leads the entire service.

"We wanted to bring a different perspective to the worship," says Wendy Golter, chairperson. "We work to include the congregation actively — more than just sitting, listening, and singing." Each fifth Sunday is different.

- One featured a slide show on God's creativity, with readings from the Psalms.
- Another centered on giving the first fruits; worshipers were asked to fill out gift certificates for their services (everything from baby-sitting to scissors sharpening), which were then exchanged with one another.
- Another was mostly musical: they sang through the life of Christ in hymns.

"We brief the pastor in advance on what we're going to do," Golter adds, "but because of a trusting atmosphere, we're free to experiment."

Family Night at the Bible church in downstate Eureka, Illinois, means one or two families leading an evening service.

"Once a month we give them charge of a Sunday night," says Pastor John Erwin. "Families have come up with special music, Scripture readings, and presentations of poems or other literature. They lead congregational singing, Bible quizzes and drills, name-that-tune contests, and many other kinds of things that kids enjoy as well as adults.

"It's proven to be a very good time of involvement as well as variety in worship, and it has also increased attendance."

The People Preach on Psalm-Day

Occasionally both the pastor and the people enjoy a break from a steady diet of sermons. At the Church of the Nazarene in Wyoming, Illinois, Pastor Ronald Compton provides the change of pace by having the entire congregation write a psalm during the normal sermon slot.

After reading Psalm 34 and explaining its acrostic

pattern (verse 1 begins with the first Hebrew letter, *aleph;* verse 2 with the second letter, *beth;* and so on), Compton had his congregation write a psalm following the same pattern in English.

"I prepared overhead transparencies with the alphabet written vertically along the left margin," says Compton. "To give some direction, I suggested the first nine verses be statements of praise, the second eight verses be requests, and the last nine verses statements of trust or praise."

Then opening up the service to anyone who thought of a line, Compton proceeded through the alphabet, writing the psalm on the transparencies.

"I was surprsied how quickly the children got into the act," says Compton. "They gave as many lines as the adults did. In fact, for the tough letters — Q, X, and Z — it was the children who came up with:

"Quite a Savior you are."

"Xylophones ring with your praise."

"Zeal fills my heart because you are God."

Upon completion, Compton read the psalm aloud as the "sermon" for the day.

"They were amazed at how real it sounded," says Compton. "The climax was when they saw their psalm printed in the following Sunday's bulletin."

Toward Better Eulogies

An old, rather morbid joke tells about the widow who checked the casket one last time to make sure it still contained her irksome husband, despite the minister's glowing remarks. Robert Hill, pastor of Westminster Presbyterian Church in Yakima, Washington, takes special care to be well informed about the deceased by gently interviewing relatives and taking notes.

Here are some of the questions he uses:

1. What one adjective would you use to describe him/her?

2. Did he have any particular loves or hobbies?

3. Did he enjoy any particular songs, poems, or Scriptures?

4. If you could name one value or lesson he most wanted to teach the next generation, what would it be?

5. What one achievement or accomplishment would make his eyes light up when you mentioned it?

6. What were some of his favorite phrases or sayings?

7. Did he ever put anything up on the wall — a picture, a motto, a clipping that expresses who he really was?

8. Did he like his first name? Did he have any nicknames?

9. Was there a cause or movement that he felt deeply about and supported with time and finances?

10. If he could have me say one thing during the funeral, what do you think it would be?

11. Why do you think this world is a little different because of him?

"I pay particular attention to the adjectives and verbs that people use," says Hill. "And I make sure that if I use any direct quotations in the eulogy, I have the person's permission.

"It's true that God is the focus of the funeral service, not the deceased. But the responses to these questions can be used to weave together illustrations of the promises found in the Bible, so that the person is honored at the same time as God's character is proclaimed."

Adapted with permission from The Clergy Journal

The Sing-along Sermon

When Tom Lorimer decided to preach on music in worship not long ago, he did more than talk about the subject. He led his congregation, Kempton Church of the Nazarene in Illinois, in an experience that blended actual singing with what the New Testament says about it.

"We opened the service with prayer and only one hymn," says Lorimer. "Then I began the message right away, based on Ephesians 5:18-20. Along the way, we stopped six different times to sing or listen to music that illustrated my points." Examples

- *Hymns in worship:* "How Firm a Foundation"
- *Instrumental praise:* the offertory
- *Music to edify those who listen:* a special number
- A *"spiritual song"* of testimony: "Redeemed"

"The message was well received and was a nice change in our usual service pattern," Lorimer says. "Naturally, any church can select songs to fit its own tradition for this kind of sermon."

An Application a Day . . .

J. L. Rivera has a confession: "As preachers, we are notorious for telling people *what* they should do. But few of us have mastered the art of effectively showing *how* to practice what we're preaching."

Recently at Christian Fellowship Church in Chicago, Rivera began a unique way of emphasizing application in his sermons.

"To aid the creative juices of people in the congregation, I compile a weekly list of potential ways this sermon could be applied in individual lives," Rivera says. The mimeographed list is then passed out to the 65-70 Sunday morning attenders as they leave the service.

"This differs from the common practice of supplying a sermon outline in the bulletin," says Rivera. "This focuses not on *content* but *application*. It's a final reminder and reinforcement."

After a recent sermon on "Characteristics of a Growing Church" from Acts 2:42-47, for example, the list included:

- *Commit yourself to attend all church services for a pe-*

riod of three months. At the end of that period, evaluate the
results of your commitment.

● *Give something you are not using to someone you
know could use it (for example, an extra umbrella, coat,
etc.).*

● *Make it a point to compliment someone else in the
body.*

● *Commit yourself to joining in worship and praise
regardless of the response you "think" you'll get from those
around you.*

"Weeks later, says Rivera, "people have mentioned
trying one or more of the practical aids. As a result, their
comments are specific rather than just a polite general
compliment about the preaching."

A Clear Invitation

Imagine the confusion. You're attending a church
service for the first time. After the sermon, the minister
hastily "offers an invitation" to"come forward and accept Jesus," and then people begin singing.

If you're not familiar with revivalistic tradition,
chances are you don't know what's happening. Asking
people to leave their seats before the program is over,
walk to the front of the auditorium, and talk to a
stranger about spiritual things is alien to anyone
accustomed to sitting passively through movies and
concerts.

That's why Gordon MacDonald, at Grace Chapel in
Lexington, Massachusetts, explains what an invitation is
before he starts his sermon.

"Whenever I'm planning to have people respond
publicly," he says, "I tell them, 'In about 30 minutes, I'm
going to ask you to do something unusual. I'll be asking you to make a decision based on the information in
today's sermon. At the end of the service, I'll invite
you to come and kneel on the steps of the platform as a
sign of God working in your life.'

"I want them to get ready, and this takes a lot of the shock, the fear, and the worry out of the experience. I explain what I want them to do as if I'd never seen an altar call before," he says.

MacDonald does this perhaps 12 times a year, usually as a public sign of conversion, and he's been doing it this way for 10 years.

"We've found that preparing people beforehand brings a greater response," he says. "People think about what they must do throughout the sermon, and when they do come forward, they mean business."

Tough Questions from Active Minds

Strong preaching has long been a hallmark in black churches, but at Oak Cliff Bible Fellowship in Dallas, Pastor Tony Evans makes sure the communication is more than one-way. He builds a 15-minute question-and-answer session into each Sunday morning service.

"Our church started from scratch in 1976, and 50 percent of our people are new converts within the last two years," says Evans of his 450-member, racially mixed congregation. He felt the need to find out what people were thinking and make sure his messages were getting through.

So after the sermon, the invitation, and the offering, Evans asks for questions about the morning message. Queries range from the doctrinal to the intensely practical.

- "If Jonah hadn't repented in the belly of the fish, would he still have been a believer?"
- "If God is stronger than Satan, why does he allow the battle to go on?"
- "1 Peter 3 talks about wives winning their husbands to the Lord by living pure, reverent lives. What if you've tried that, and your husband gets worse instead of better?"

- "What can you do if you've already failed with your children because you didn't know good Christian principles of child-raising when the kids were young?"

"Of course," says Evans, "you've got to know what you're talking about. I was fortunate enough to have a good solid theological education, but every once in a while I still get an unanswerable question, like 'How can a being such as God not have a beginning?' Some answers can't be put into human language. But I'd still rather have the questions asked than bottled up inside."

Rick Yohn, pastor of the large Evangelical Free Church of Fresno, California, believes in letting his people set the Sunday night agenda occasionally.

"A couple of times each year," he says, "I don't preach — I just respond to written questions from the congregation. Three weeks in advance, we begin announcing that questions are welcome — anything on anyone's mind."

Yohn sometimes garners as many as 40-50 questions and spends more than one service answering them. They run a wide gamut, from "How do you keep your preaching notes from falling out of your Bible?" (he uses a rubber band) to serious doctrinal matters:

"Can I lose my salvation?"

"When do you think Christ is coming back?"

"What is appropriate conduct for a divorcee?"

"Is abortion wrong, and if so, why?"

Yohn has Ask-the-Pastor Night "whenever I sense there are unspoken questions out there, a slight restlessness or curiosity. It helps me stay close to their genuine concerns and interests."

Listening to the Listeners

"What does the board really think of my preaching?" Robert Olson is one pastor who decided to do more than worry about that question; he found out.

After 14 years of ministry at Memorial Park Baptist Church in Vestal, New York, Olson gave each board member a questionnaire to fill out anonymously. A list of more than 20 questions asked for feedback on such areas as sermon length, content, delivery, timeliness, impact of illustrations, biblical usage, recent themes, even humor.

"I wanted to know what they were thinking but not saying," he explains. "When the forms came in, I got more support and confirmation than I had expected. I was willing to receive constructive criticisms, but actually, there were only one or two. And they were helpful.

"As a result, I felt a greater sense of confidence in my preaching."

Olson expects to do this kind of survey about every five years, just to stay in touch with a strategic group of listeners.

WORSHIP

Time Out to Worship

"Be still and know that I am God" is a Scripture more quoted than implemented on Sunday morning. The rush to get a family up, fed, dressed, and driven to church is often not eased until the afternoon snooze.

At High Road Bible Church in Romeoville, Illinois, there's a major block of time in the morning service each week for silent prayer and worship. After announcements, responsive reading, and an opening hymn comes a recorded selection from "Praise Strings," which runs from 3½ to 5 minutes. "This lets people truly unwind, slow down, and reflect on the One they've come to worship," says Pastor Matthew Heard.

Each week Heard suggests a different psalm as a point of focus, to pray or read back to the Lord. "This helps new Christians learn to praise him, gives visitors something definite to do, and is enjoyed by more mature Christians as well," he says. At the end, he leads the congregation into a sharing time — praise items, reflections on the psalm just noted, requests and needs, then the pastoral prayer.

"The feedback has been entirely positive," says the pastor, looking back over the year since the silent worship time began. Often it's the first thing visitors compliment after the service: "That was a breath of fresh air." "We've never been to a church where they gave time for this before."

Key factor: The music that sets the mood must be instrumental, not vocal. The style, obviously, needs to be reflective rather than upbeat. "The five 'Praise Strings' albums have been ideal for us," says Heard, "and it's been no problem to repeat various selections at times.

"However, one Sunday our sound system was out, so I asked our organist to prepare something appropriate instead. This worked just as well."

Worship 101: In-the-Pew Training

Do Christians automatically know how to worship?

Not necessarily, says John Walden, Sr., pastor of Faith Baptist Church, Binghampton, New York. That is why he's been taking the first five minutes of the Sunday morning service to teach about various elements of worshiping God. Different weeks have dealt with such themes as:

- A worship experience is not what you get, but what you give.
- How to *prepare* for worship — privately, during the week.
- The place of congregational singing: why the first hymn, for example, is always a song of adoration rather than testimony.
- How to worship during the choir's singing rather than just watch a performance.
- The importance of Scripture reading in a public service.
- The reason for a sermon.

"I have to work hard to keep it short," says Walden, "so it doesn't balloon into an additional morning message. I hit just one concept and then say, 'Now, as we worship today, here is what will happen and why. You'll notice your bulletin says we are going to do such-and-such, and the reason is . . .' Then comes the call to worship, and the service begins."

Response from this congregation of 300 has been strong. Many have said things like "You've helped me understand what worship really is."

As for Walden, he has been going for a full year and

sees no reason to stop. "I'll do this as long as I preach," he says, "because the congregation keeps changing. Occasionally, I say, 'If this sounds familiar to you, remember that many didn't hear it the last time.'

"Training people to truly worship is an ongoing process. And it's paying off in the attitudes of both new and older Christians."

Preview of a Coming Attraction

At the large First United Methodist Church in Fort Worth, Texas, worshipers' appetites are whetted for the sermon by a quick foretaste halfway through the service.

Right after the pastoral prayer, Senior Minister Barry Bailey gives a two-minute capsule of what he will preach later on. A thesis sentence is followed by a few of the main ideas, but without giving away any surprise elements. Listeners say it's like reading a synopsis of a play before the curtain rises; it helps their understanding of what's to follow but doesn't divulge the outcome.

Bailey, who has done capsules throughout his ministry, including the last six years at this church, points to another benefit. "It makes me state what I plan to preach about in a few words — which is good discipline for any preacher."
Reported by Harold Glen Brown

A Glimpse of Things to Come

If a church doesn't have a Sunday night tradition (and even if it does), getting people to attend Sunday evening events can be a challenge.

When the United Methodist Church in Coralville, Iowa, decided to have a six-week film series, a lay person's creative suggestion helped make it a success.

"Promoting films through printed or verbal announcements didn't adequately capture the power of the evening film," says George White, who was pastor at the time. "Someone suggested showing a clip of the film during the morning service."

Each week a particularly interesting one or two-minute segment of that night's film was previewed during morning worship.

The result? Sunday evening attendance for the series averaged 150, compared with a normal 30-50.

"The Sunday morning film clip doesn't get all the credit," says White. "The high quality of the films, community-wide publicity, and personal invitations also were factors. But the previews did contribute to the strong response."

USING ELECTRONIC MEDIA IN WORSHIP

by Mel White, film maker and former pastor,
Evangelical Covenant Church, Pasadena, California

"What a gimmick, Mel," jibed my friend-critic-fellow pastor, "using all that electronic media in worship. No wonder your crowd is growing."

I bit my tongue. How often I had heard that good-natured questioning of my liturgical methods and motives. "Just show biz," he might have added. Or worse, "Just an easy way to keep from preparing a sermon."

Wrong on both counts. My motive for using electronic media in worship is the same as for every hymn, prayer, or sermon: to lift up Christ and draw his people one step closer to him and to each other. And the method is not a short cut. It is time-consuming and risky. (And never have I eliminated the sermon with media, only supplemented and supported it.) When you spend valuable time, energy, and money to integrate a one-minute film clip only to have an usher trip on the plug mid-screening and plunge the church into darkness, or when the slide bearing the words to the morning anthem pops on upside-down, you wonder if using media is worth the impugning of your motives.

But believe me, it's worth it. The excitement people feel, the enthusiasm with which old-timers invite friends and family to worship, and the changed lives and renewed spirits can be traced, at least in part, to God's Spirit at work in and through electronic worship aids.

My wife, Lyla, our director of worship, and our worship

team (volunteers with interest if not expertise in media, art, music, and liturgy) integrated two types of media into morning worship: (1) *sight* (16mm film, 8mm film, video tape, slide projections, and lighting) and (2) *sound* (records and audio cassettes). For the sake of brevity we must skip over the use of media in the Sunday evening service and the educational or outreach programs of the church and get down to each medium, with a couple of ideas that worked for us in worship.

1. *16mm film.* I use very short films in worship. (The new high-intensity lamps and rear-screen projection systems allow for use of media even in churches once thought impossible to darken.) One- or two-minute spots, for example, the Franciscan teleketic spots, are wonderful calls to worship, introductions to a hymn or reading, thought-provoking "secular lessons," perfect sermon setups, or final benedictions. Or, use a brief portion of a longer film, for example "The Ping Pong Ball" parable from *Why Men Create* (Pyramid Films) or the Crucifixion or Resurrection scenes from a great christological film, for example *The Gospel Road* (World Wide Pictures).

The problem? You can't use a film you don't know about. The resources are limited only by your knowledge of what's available. That's why it's so valuable to get the various catalogues through your local film distributor (or directly from the national film distributors), to visit your local film library to meet and get ideas from librarians, and to appoint a search team of film buffs in your congregation to find the resources for use in worship.

2. *8mm film.* Make your own films for worship. Interpret a biblical passage, a hymn, or a great historic moment from the church calendar. Never let Christmas or Easter or Pentecost pass without assigning a class or committee, even a children's group, to create an 8mm film clip for worship. Our junior high department's version of Christ's return to the disciples in the Upper Room after the Crucifixion (they

were wearing bathrobes and eating McDonald's burgers) turned out to be humorous, whimsical, and poignant beyond belief. Brief productions in 8mm featuring your people expressing their faith in literal or impressionistic ways will add a dimension to worship that few professionally produced films can beat.

3. *Video tape projections.* One of the fastest selling electronic appliances in the nation is the home video projection unit. Soon, portable life-size video projection systems will be available to every church. (We borrow them from families in the church now.) So now you can have all the wonderful advantages of scenes from the great films only available through video. For example, Gospel Films (Box 455, Muskegon, MI 49443) is now renting cheaply such easily adapted films as Zeffirelli's *Jesus of Nazareth* or *Chariots of Fire.* Too, with the inexpensive color video cameras popping up in people's homes, we can produce interviews, testimonies, prayer requests, special music, and drama for worship at almost no cost.

4. *Slides.* I found our use of slides to be the simplest and most helpful electronic worship tool. We required the photo company that made our church directory to provide us with a slide of every member of the church. We projected slides when a new member was being introduced or when a prayer request was being made. Remember, we have people who have worshiped side by side for twenty-five years and still don't know one another's names. To see those pictures gives worth and honor to the person on the screen and helps the rest of us know who it is we're praying for.

5. *Light.* I despise house lights on dimmers that go up when we take the offering and down when we pray. But when a single spotlight or candle lights up the chalice and the loaf, or the great pulpit Bible (while Scripture is read over the amplification system), or a banner, or the cross, it helps people quietly focus and listen and worship.

6. *Records.* I believe we should use our own people to

sing and read in worship. But now and again the Christian recording industry (and occasionally the secular) produces recorded music and effects that are perfect for worship. To discover Ken Medema's song about the church — "If this is not a place where my tears are understood, where can I go to cry?" — and to project slides of our church at worship was to have an incredible worship experience. Once I began a sermon by simply standing in the pulpit and playing Peggy Lee's "Is That All There Is?" as an opening illustration. Though "secular," people didn't forget it or the sermon that followed.

7. *Cassette tapes*. We can make up our own tapes for replay in worship. For example, my sermon theme was "The Sounds of the Morning" (a look at Jesus' habit of stealing away before dawn to pray). I asked a young woman with a good recorder to climb the hills above Pasadena and record the sounds of the morning (coyotes, dogs barking, wind in the trees, leaves rustling). For the worship prelude, we played those sounds and projected slides of a sunrise. Unforgettable and appropriate.

Lyla and I don't do all this ourselves. Our worship committee is invaluable. I wish I could share all the things they did with the themes and texts I gave them two months in advance. Often I would sit waiting to preach and be so moved by what they had done that I had to dry the tears before I could speak. Besides the worship experience they provided us, it was a chance for our people to exercise their gifts in worship. Often people in the pew, asked to be spectators at worship year after year, are drying up, bored and uninvolved, simply because they've not been asked to dream. Our worship group, given titles and texts in advance and set free to communicate them, amazed us. What they created brought new life, health, and serendipity to worship.

MUSIC

Learning to Love
a New Hymnal

More than one church has had a fight on its hands
trying to change hymnals. The old books may lack the
contemporary tunes, but they retain a lot of warm
feelings that many members cherish.

First Christian Church of Hayward, California,
smoothed the way recently by having its choir woo the
congregation for several Sundays with new songs
from the new hymnbook prior to formal introduction.
After the committee had done its research and made
its choice, "we took our time creating an awareness of
what could be gained by changing over," says Pastor
James B. Fenderson. "We ordered only 30 new hymnals
at first — just enough for the choir to use."

Each Sunday another new hymn would be featured.
The 30 hymnals were also passed out at a weekly potluck
supper for members to peruse. Inevitably singing began, with such enthusiasm that "I finally had to cut it
off," Fenderson remembers.

Soon the education process was complete. The order for 120 more copies of the new book was sent off,
and "we now have a lot of new hymns that express
what our hearts mean to say in these times," reports the
pastor.

When the Organist
Is Away

With a little ingenious wiring, the Tempe Seventh-
day Adventist Church in Arizona enjoys organ music
even when the organist is out of town.

"We were remodeling the church," says Pastor Ervin K. Thomsen, "and so I took the opportunity to install a direct line from the organ" (an Allen Digital Computer model) "to the PA console. I also put in a remote control near the pulpit to govern the reel-to-reel tape recorder."

The result: organ music can be recorded with great fidelity and replayed at will through the organ speaker system.

Thomsen, an organist himself, tells what happened one weekend when the church organist called in sick and no substitute could be found. "I simply went to the church the night before and recorded the entire service — prelude, congregational hymns, offertory, postlude. The next morning I was able to provide everything at the proper time with just a flip of the switch as I led the service."

Naturally, some worshipers were surprised to hear music with no one at the console. But it was certainly better than an organ-less service.

"I can think of other ways to use the system," Thomsen adds. "Organists leaving for vacation could prerecord services to be used while they're gone. They could also provide tapes to small churches that lack qualified organists."

HELP FOR WEAK CONGREGATIONAL SINGING

by Dale McClure, minister of music, South Evangelical Presbyterian Fellowship, Englewood, Colorado

After four weeks, Jim knew something was wrong. The people in the "daughter" church weren't singing like they had in the old congregation.

Jim was the lay music director of our mission church. A month earlier we had begun the new congregation with 80 people, and already the attendance was over 100.

They had one problem, however — weak congregational singing. Many of Jim's members were the same people who had participated in the exhilarating worship at the mother church. There, enthusiastic singing seemed easy and natural.

"It's not the same," he said one day on his lunch hour. "What can I do?"

As we talked over burgers and fries, we discovered that what we did at the mother church of 800 could be done with his 100. In fact, these principles could be adapted to almost any congregation to encourage better singing.

First, good congregational singing starts with the congregation knowing why they are singing.

Each Sunday we determine if the purpose of the service is worship, instruction, fellowship, or evangelism. While all these functions of the body of Christ may overlap or may sometimes occur simultaneously, we try to focus on one or two functions. After we have determined the function, we make sure that everything in the service supports the function — including the congregational singing.

If our goal is worship, then our congregational singing will be songs of praise, adoration, or thanksgiving. If our goals is instruction, then we choose songs that amplify and reinforce the particular biblical doctrine or principle for the day. If our goal is fellowship, then the content of the songs is not nearly as important as whether the people enjoy singing them. If the goal for the service is evangelism, we choose songs that proclaim the gospel in a manner easily understood by unbelievers.

And in the service, either at the outset in a statement from the pulpit, or while introducing the songs, or in the printed bulletin, we tell the congregation why and to whom we are singing these particular songs.

Educating our congregation to the purpose of the service, how their singing relates to that purpose, and to whom they are to sing are the first steps toward good singing

The second thing that contributes to strong congregational singing is clear leadership.

The leader needs to be visible. Whether we use a single songleader, a leader playing an instrument, or a full choir and orchestra, visibility is important. By seeing the leadership, the congregation responds better then to an unknown source from behind a screen, from an organ well, or from a balcony.

The leader must be audible. For the nonmusician in the pew, it is not enough to see a conductor. The songleader needs to sing. I was a composition major, not a vocalist. My voice teacher said my voice was made for cooling soup. I will never be a soloist, but I use my voice to lead our congregation to better singing.

If the leader's voice is weak, use a microphone. If you lead from a piano, organ, or some other instrument, make sure your voice can be heard above it. If a choir is leading, make sure they are audible. The leader needs to give clear signals as to tempo, starts, and stops. The leader should use standard conducting patterns if possible.

Nonmusicians in the congregation are more comfortable about what to do when they follow a leader. It is much easier to follow when that leadership is clearly understood, easily heard, and highly visible.

A third important contribution is good accompaniment.

Good accompaniment starts with the introduction, which should establish the key, set the tempo, and remind those who don't read music of the tune. Long or elaborate introductions are seldom necessary. Two to eight measures (first and last phrases) are usually sufficient.

We vary the instrumental accompaniment often, using instruments other than piano and organ. For instance, we use classical guitar and flute for "Blest Be the Tie That Binds" and folk guitar for "Jesus, Name Above All Names." We use a full rhythm section (drums, bass guitar, rhythm guitar, and percussion) when we sing "The Lord Is Good." Our string quartet accompanies us when we sing "Jesus, the Very Thought of Thee" and "Oh, How He Loves You and Me." The brass section is a natural for "All Hail the Power of Jesus' Name" and "And Can It Be." Our congregation loves to sing with a full orchestra; therefore, we assemble one often. Our people are most enthusiastic when the timpani roll, the violins are playing above the staff, the cymbals crash, and the woodwinds trill on "Crown Him with Many Crowns." It often moves me to the point of visualizing what it will be like with Jesus.

We sing *a capella,* too. No instruments accompany us when we sing "Fairest Lord Jesus" or "I Love You, Lord, and I Lift My Voice."

Accompaniments for various instrumental combinations are available from several different publishers. We have purchased and use the orchestrations for *Great Hymns of the Faith* from Singspiration. We also like the instrumental edition of *Baptist Hymnal* from Convention Press. Lillenas publishes *500 Hymns for Instruments* as well as an orchestration to their *Praise and Worship* hymnal. I write many of our own orchestrations so that our particular combination of instruments will be used to the best advantage.

A fourth thing that has helped our singing is the use of special arrangements for the congregation.

I often make very simple arrangements by putting together medleys of related choruses, making modulations within a song, reharmonizing a last stanza, or adding a descant.

For example, we sing "The Lord Is Good," "God Is So Good," and "Great Is Thy Faithfulness" in medley — all in the key of D. Sometimes we add a second chorus of "Great Is Thy Faithfulness" in E-flat. We almost always make a key change on the last stanza of "Amazing Grace" and "Jesus Paid It All." The reharmonizations are printed in *Hymns for the Family of God* from Paragon.

The same hymnal is a good source of descants. On a last stanza, try having the congregation sing the melody while sopranos and tenors in the choir sing a descant. Descants can also be found in *Festive Descants for Joyful Worship* from Lexicon Music, and *Descants for Choir* from Lillenas. An easy way of creating your own descant is to have the sopranos in the choir sing the tenor part up one octave. Descants can create excitement in the singing.

Since our congregation is accustomed to all these "weird" changes, they tackle even more difficult things like published choir works. They have sung along with the choir every time we have done the finale to the Gaithers' *Alleluia.* They have almost memorized Handel's "Hallelujah Chorus." We have sung two medleys from *Hymns Triumphant* and several selections from the *Praise III* and *Praise IV* choral collections. They also sing the congregational parts in Ronn Huff's *Exaltation.* All these more complex arrangements have met with avid interest and excellent participation even though they were originally meant for choirs. We simply print the lyrics in our bulletins (with permission from the publishers if they are copyrighted) or buy preprinted song sheets and have the choir lead. Then after a few times through, everyone is singing.

Perhaps most important for strong congregational singing, however, is that the people know their singing is important.

A congregation can sense how important their leaders think singing is by how much time and energy is put into its preparation. Because we make such a production of the congregation's singing, they know we value it.

If leaders have the attitude that the choral anthems and solos are the truly important pieces of music, the congregation will feel it. If the music leadership feels that the anthems and solos support and lead up to the congregation's music, then the people will respond with more energy.

How congregational singing is used will communicate its importance to the congregation. When it is used as "filler" or as an opportunity to stand and stretch or to get people settled or started, people will sing with little enthusiasm. When congregational singing is used purposefully, people will put forth much more effort.

This is shown by where the congregational singing is placed in the service. It is not unusual for one of our worship services to have everything (sermon included) lead up to when the people rise and loudly sing praises to God. When it is the focal point of the service, our people know it is important.

Jim and I talked about other things, like the choice of a good hymnal, using sources other than the hymnal, the effect of acoustics, the importance of seating people close together, and rehearsing a congregation. We also talked about how much time it takes to develop a singing church. All the talking made our hamburgers cold and the french fries limp, but it was worth it. The ideas began working for him just like they worked for us.

Singers for Supper

When Jerry and Jeannie Herbert wanted to make college students and other singles feel more welcome in the choir they led, they came up with a novel enticement: potluck dinner at their house an hour before each Wednesday night rehearsal.

"We lived just a few blocks from the church," (Blacknall Presbyterian in Durham, North Carolina) says Jerry, who's since moved away, "and we just opened our home to whoever wanted to show up. At first we footed the bill, but soon the group began volunteering to bring a salad, vegetable, or main dish the following week. While it was mostly Duke University people and career types in the beginning, some young marrieds began coming as well."

A large piece of plywood was hauled out each week to rest atop the smaller dining table and thus accommodate more plates. "We really began to feel part of a group," Sue Price, one of the altos, remembers. "We got very close to Jerry and Jeannie and sensed we were bound together in a common ministry."

As many as 20 of the 30 choir members eventually came for the potlucks, which went on for a full two years. "It was an opportunity to get to know the other person as more than just a tenor or a soprano," says Jerry. "It was crowded, but fun." Only when the choir membership underwent a change, with a number of students moving on and some couples becoming parents, did the weekly meals stop one May and not resume in September.

"But it was a *good* idea," says Dave Stuntz, Blacknall's current director of music, "and we're thinking now about how to revive it. Instead of using a nearby home, for example, we might move it to the church's kitchen. We need the togetherness that this kind of thing builds."

Let ALL the People Praise

For every person in the choir loft, there's probably someone else in the pew who would like to sing, is qualified — but can't promise to be there every week.

To tap that kind of talent, First Evangelical Covenant Church in Rockford, Illinois, started a once-a-month "Praise Choir." To join, you don't sign any long-range commitment; you only show up for a one-hour rehearsal on the Wednesday evening before the last Sunday of the month.

"On that Sunday, our usual Chancel Choir of 35 is suddenly twice as large," says Pastor Richard Johnson. "They dispense with robes, and they sing mainly praise-oriented music — simple, singable arrangements that can be prepared quickly and still sound very acceptable.

"There's an excitement about their music; the spirit of this choir has become contagious throughout the congregation."

A side benefit over the past year has been that four or five Praise Choir singers have enjoyed it so much they've decided to join the regular choir. Others who would like to join but have conflicting ministries — workers in the youth clubs, for example (which meet simultaneously with the choir on Wednesday nights) — are excused this night each month in order to rehearse with the Praise Choir.

"We've also uncovered some new soloists and duet combinations," Johnson adds. "It has been an excellent way to broaden the ministry of music in the church."

Growing Your Own Orchestra

A Decatur, Georgia, church has stopped taking chances that the schools and private teachers will automatically train the skilled musicians it needs.

Chapel Hill Harvester Church offers *free* string, brass, woodwind, and percussion lessons to its children, taught by members of the congregation.

"Our people really have a desire to serve the Lord," says Clariece Paulk, minister of arts and music, "and so we have six different people who give of their time every Wednesday night to teach. That's their ministry to the body." One is a high school band director; another teaches music at a Christian academy.

From 25 to 30 young students are currently enrolled, some as young as seven. Beginners are often clustered for group instruction, but more advanced students get individual attention. The lessons are offered as an option to the church's graded choir program, which runs on Wednesday night as well. Other parts of the evening include Bible classes and recreation.

"Since we began giving lessons," Paulk adds, "people in the church have been moved to donate idle instruments, so we're often able to meet that need as well. Sometimes the timing has been amazing. A person handed me a flute one morning, and that very evening a mother mentioned her daughter's interest in the flute. 'Guess what someone brought me just today!' I said."

Thanks to the lessons, the children's Alpha Orchestra is able to play in children's church once a month, in the main worship service six or seven times a year, and will soon add nursing homes and other outreaches as well.

A Crowd to Practice On

How do you get choir members to take dress rehearsals seriously?

As every conductor knows, some aspects of excellence are mastered only under the pressure of facing a live audience. But if the first live audience is the one at the actual performance — it's too late.

That's why the adult choir at Berwick Church of Christ outside Melbourne, Australia, decided to import an audience for its dress rehearsals — from nearby nursing homes. "Each time we were ready to present a cantata we contacted administrators of the various homes to see who would like to attend," explains Pastor Norval Bunch, who now serves a church in Bellingham, Washington. "Then spouses of choir members and others from the church would go pick them up for the occasion."

The advantages were many:

- The choir instinctively worked harder in the dress rehearsal.
- The elderly got to enjoy a musical presentation without worrying about either transportation or crowds.
- Families of choir members had a way to support the ministry.
- Since refreshments were served to everyone afterward, good fellowship resulted.
- Others in the community got involved. The owner of a bus company heard about the plan and offered to pick up residents in the future.

"The idea benefited the choir and was an outreach at the same time," says the pastor.

They Sang What?

It's a known fact that audiences frequently miss many of the choir's lyrics on Sunday morning. Either the musical embellishments get in the way, or the words themselves are garbled, or the listener is daydreaming, or . . .

The choir at Church of the New Covenant in Vacaville, California, got to talking one rehearsal about the visual images in the hymn being practiced. "We found ourselves describing mountains, rivers — various scenes we had visited on vacation," says Colleen Britton. "The words suddenly came alive and were very personal for each of us. How could we share this with the congregation?"

By Sunday they had put together a homemade slide show to illustrate each phrase of the song. "We combined our slides from various family outings and trips, and it was beautiful," she says. "The congregation focused intently on what we were singing; they were totally involved with the hymn.

This kind of treatment works easiest, of course, with repertoire about Creation. The Vacaville choir has done slide shows to accompany "God Who Touches Earth with Beauty," "All Things Bright and Beautiful," "This Is My Father's World," "All Creatures of Our God and King," and "For the Beauty of the Earth." But other subjects can be developed as well.

"We've used the technique effectively both in worship and church school classes, " says Britton.

Where Special Requests Are Special

Most churchgoers like the chance to request favorite hymns — but end up choosing the same dozen songs again and again, often because of their lively tunes rather than their texts.

Pastor Lawrence Roff has several ways to beat that problem. At Fairfield Presbyterian Church in Fairton, New Jersey, where request time is part of each Sunday evening service, he has successfully used the following:

• Assign someone to research a well-known (but not threadbare) hymn and give a brief report in the service. "I loan books from my library that tell details about the author and composer, the hymn's period of church history, interesting events about its composition, doctrinal or literary highlights in the text," says the pastor. "We do this especially for Christmas carols."

- Announce that each person requesting a hymn must add why he or she wishes to have it sung. This may relate to a key life event, a striking reference to a doctrine, or a devotional theme. One woman who lost both her mother and father within a three-week period, for example, had good reason on the one-year anniversary of their deaths to request "Whate'er My God Ordains Is Right."

- Occasionally feature a theme — "Tonight let's choose only psalm settings" or "hymns about the holiness of God," or providence, or the Second Coming. For other evenings Roff has guided choices to a certain writer: Watts, Wesley, or Luther.

"A new appreciation for the richness of church music is growing in the congregation," says the pastor. "People are getting beyond catchy melodies to content."

A Shopper's Guide to Wedding Music

Question: When making wedding plans, on which subject are the bride and groom least informed but most opinionated?

Likely answer: music. Most couples want to give it their individual touch but have little background to guide them. However, they did hear this neat Barry Manilow song on the radio. . . .

One pastor who's found a way to focus the discussion within bounds and also save time is James Schackel, Zion Lutheran Church, Montrose, Colorado. "We're in a small town, and our resources are limited," he says. "So I asked DeLoy Goeglein, organist at one of our larger sister churches in the Denver area, to help us. He recorded an assortment of better wedding music within the range of our organists and the capabilities of our organ."

Schackel then made a dozen duplicates of the tape for loaning to engaged couples. Meanwhile, the Zion organists began acquiring the printed scores for Goeglein's selections.

"This saves countless hours for everybody — the couple, myself, and the organist who must otherwise come to the church to demonstrate the options," says the pastor. "They simply listen to the tape on their own and then let us know their choices."

A Quiet Understanding

To help soloists and music groups know what's expected, choir director Terry White of Wooddale Church in suburban Minneapolis sends an information sheet several weeks in advance.

The one-page form, called "So You're Going to Sing at Wooddale . . ." has blanks for White to fill in the service date, the time, and the sermon topic and Bible text. The sheet has proved "highly successful," especially with visiting musicians, he says.

Although he inherited the idea from his predecessor, White has expanded and revised the form to cover such areas as

● contacting accompanists

● what to wear (robes for morning services but not at night)

● use of photocopied music ("We don't do it — if you can't find a second copy for the accompanist, please let me know in time to buy another copy.")

● prefacing a musical number with talking ("Our pastor is here to speak — you're here to sing.")

● communicative suggestions ("Please use ranging eye contact; memorize the music or bring words on three-by-five cards to the pulpit.")

Visiting musicians, White says, have repeatedly thanked him for the clear guidelines and expectations.

Easy on the Eardrums

How do you keep a visiting musical group's volume level under control?

Central Tabernacle in Edmonton has solved that problem once and for all with a firm policy: groups may bring in as many microphones, amps, and sound men as they like, but the final mix will be put through the house speakers, with the church's sound operator (a layman) controlling the volume.

"Naturally, some of the groups are a little disgruntled at first," says Laurey Berteig, minister of music, "but they don't have to take the criticism if the audience is uncomfortable. They can leave town the next day.

"This way, there are no ugly scenes, no whispered arguments about whether something is too loud, no need for apologies at the end of a concert. We know what our people are comfortable with, and the policy insures that their limits will not be breached."

It doesn't hurt, of course, that Central Tabernacle is a desirable booking for groups on the road. With 1,500 in attendance on an average Sunday, it's the second largest church in its denomination (Pentecostal Assemblies of Canada). "Over the years, we've had them all," says Bertieg " — the Imperials, Truth, Regeneration, Doug Oldham, Andrus Blackwood, Lillie Knauls, Tom Netherton, and many others. They've all conformed to the policy.

"I tell them, 'Look, our sound man is very flexible and, if anything, tends to run the system a little hot as it is. So you're not going to be cramped. I understand your need to mix your own sound, since you know your voicing and your material — that's fine. And if your sound man is amiable and cooperative, our policy isn't going to make much difference in the end.' "

The only exceptions over the past ten years have been when the church neglected to inform the artist in advance. 'You can't spring this on a group at the last minute," says Bertieg. "But with good planning, you can have top-name music and still protect yourself from criticism."

ENERGIZING WORSHIP: A TEAM APPROACH

by Jonathan W. Bergt, minister of music, Washington Park
Fellowship, St. Louis, Missouri

How does the average pew-sitter who has always
assumed he's "not musical" awaken to the joys of worship
through wholehearted singing? What can inspire the 70
percent who often mumble their way through hymns?

A good precise organist helps.

In many churches, a vigorous songleader — usually
male — sets the tempo and sings out strongly.

But to modern North Americans, the organ is hardly a
popular sing-along instrument. And one man waving his arms
at a podium reminds us of the concert hall.

At Washington Park Fellowship, we didn't sit down and
analyze these limitations when we began worship teams. We
only knew we wanted *everyone* — not just the musical mi-
nority — to interact with God in worship. We were less concerned with carrying on traditions than with meeting God.

So we found ourselves evolving toward teams — small
ensembles that would lead congregational singing as a group.
They were not on the platform to perform special arrangements (although some developed those as well); their primary
task was to model worship and lead the congregation. The
combination of three or four voices and several instruments
created higher impact than a lone songleader could ever
hope for; still, each group was small enough to be flexible and
tightly synchronized.

When I became Washington Park's first minister of music in the late '70s, I began to build on what was already happening. My background was a blend of the Lutheran church, with its medieval, Renaissance, baroque, and classical styles, and some influence from various charismatic churches. Before becoming a Christian I had been in a rock band, and later on I received a college degree in classical guitar.

This church had learned, from the Jesus movement, that the guitar could function as a lead instrument. So I began leading worship teams with my guitar, the other instruments being piano, bass, and percussion, plus an obbligato instrument for color: flute, synthesizer, a woodwind, or additional guitar. We used enough singers for triadic harmonies (or even SATB for hymns), reading from hymnals when possible, improvising on the more contemporary choruses and Scripture music.

The result has been dramatic. People in the congregation feel less inhibited to join in singing; they are part of an overall sound. They see people like themselves up front, both male and female, entering into worship, and they do the same. Their models are now more than the pastoral staff and a choir in robes — who, after all, are "expected" to participate. Instead, the voices, faces, and instruments of ordinary people lead the way into the presence of God.

Such teams do not pre-empt a choir or orchestra. In fact, Washington Park currently has four choirs. Their special music is a part of worship, too — not just entertainment. But by its very nature a choir is too large to flow with the subtle nuances of guiding 15-20 minutes of continuous praise and worship.

Likewise, our 26-piece orchestra plays three times a month, twice on Sunday morning and once on Sunday evening. It has the usual mixture of music majors, experienced players, and amateurs who enjoy using their gifts to the glory of God. In addition to playing written orchestrations that enhance the choir's anthems and cantatas, the group improvises during congregational singing. The less experienced members play mostly melody, while the more experienced add chordal harmonies or obbligatos, being careful not to clutter the sound. We welcome this addition to our services.

But the focus for the average worshiper, whether skilled note reader or monotone, is on the worship team.

The team members are selected according to two important criteria:

● *Relationship with God.* This is first, not second. We base this on the Old Testament pattern of the music leaders being not just anyone with a good voice, but Levites (1 Chron. 15:16; 2 Chron. 29:25-26). They were people set apart for ministry. The congregation assumes that those seen regularly leading worship are examples to follow, and so their lives must reflect integrity before God. As David put it in Psalm 24:3-4, "Who may stand in his holy place? He who has clean hands and a pure heart. . . ."

●*Musical flexibility.* In our situation, instrumentalists need to be able to play by ear from basic chord progressions; singers must be able to find harmonies for themselves. This does not preclude advance rehearsing or planning. Before any worship service, we discuss the probable list of music to be led, along with modulations, rhythm and time signature changes, and other necessary information. New material has been rehearsed to the point that the harmonies and chord progressions are semi-memorized. So we go to the microphones with a plan.

But in Washington Park's style of worship, the plan is always subject to change. That is why each person must stay both flexible and alert. The monitor speakers of our sound system are indispensable here. The lead singer's voice and instruments are heard above the rest, and this keeps the group synchronized.

The greatest unifying factor, however, is not seen by the congregation at all. It is the team's time of prayer and worship before the service starts. We ask the Lord for guidance, but above all, we try to move our attention off ourselves and in the direction of God. Actually, we begin worshiping before the worship service begins. Once we are in the service, we simply coordinate a flow of worship that has already begun.

Obviously, problems have arisen, and some are still not completely solved. We have had to find what has an overall pleasing appearance and still allows for adequate communication between musicians. Spontaneous modulations and rhythm changes are not always completely successful, so we keep trying various visual cues and monitor adjustments.

Although we enjoy a variety of musical expressions, from the Bach and Handel of my Lutheran background, to the gospel songs of our Assemblies of God hymnal, to contemporary songs, we have not yet found a really smooth transition between styles. We want to keep worship in a continuous flow rather than breaking it up into segments. So we continue to try to work through these problems.

Worship teams are not limited to churches like ours. We have sent teams to accompany our pastors when they go to minister to other congregations, and the teams help encourage worship, teach new music, and cross denominational as well as cultural lines successfully. I have seen other, more formal churches use small groups of, say, piano, flute, guitar, and vocalists as a change from the pipe organ when teaching new hymns or when involving youth in worship.

We've also had success using teams with groups as small as 30 and as large as several thousand. The congregational response has repeatedly been positive, with comments like "There's such a special atmosphere when the group begins to sing and play — you *can't* just sit there and watch!" The more people we've involved in this form of leadership, the more our worship experience has grown.

I believe worship teams have been effective at Washington Park Fellowship not because we were trying to throw out old ways or be avant-garde, nor even because we were blending the old and the new. Rather it is because they have helped us find a freedom to worship God for who he is and to enjoy his presence together.

REACHING OUT

Faster Than a Speeding Welcome Wagon

When a family moves to Olathe, Kansas, it's not long before someone from College Church of the Nazarene welcomes them and invites them to church — usually during their first week in town.

"We've found that calling on new residents is one of the most productive ways of reaching people in the community," says Pastor Paul Cunningham. "Studies have shown that during transition points in people's lives, they're more open to change — including spiritual commitment and church involvement."

So convinced is the church of the value of new resident contacts that it hires a student from Nazarene Theological Seminary in Kansas City, 15 miles away, to do the initial calling.

"Once a week our secretary goes to the gas company to get the names of newcomers — perhaps 25 a week in our town of 40,000 — and passes them on to the seminary student," says Cunningham.

The student visits each family, welcomes them to town, gives them a brochure on College Church, invites them to attend, and gets as much information about the family as possible — number of children, ages, names, and church background. Afterwards, the student records the information onto a dictating machine in the car.

Those who show interest in the church are visited again, this time by lay volunteers on Saturday morning.

"Since the newcomers have already been visited once and have expressed an interest in the church, this takes the pressure off our Saturday volunteers," says

Cunningham. "They aren't calling cold turkey.

"The initial caller doesn't have to be a seminary student — any competent person could do it. But we've found that pay enhances the importance of the job. There's more accountability for hours worked, calls made, and information gathered. We feel it's definitely worth the cost."

More Than a Handshake

Special groups of families are responsible for greeting visitors at the Church of Christ in Cuyahoga Falls, Ohio.

These families not only welcome new people; they invite them to a dinner on the church premises, prepared by themselves, after the Sunday morning service.

"It is one program we have going that has helped our church grow by 25 percent in one year," says John Fisk, minister.

This 300-member fellowship divided its people into ten groups of families, with eight to ten families in each group. One family in each group is the "leadership family" and is responsible for coordinating the group's activities. This means positioning the greeters, coordinating the Sunday meal, and taking charge of the follow-up of visitors.

"The greeters go to different parts of the church," says Fisk. "I tell them, 'Please don't allow any new person to be overlooked. Greet them as soon as they set foot in the building!' "

Once a woman came with her children to the Sunday service, "and you could tell she wasn't expecting to be accepted," says Fisk. Before and after the service, however, the family group of that day clustered around this indigent family, introducing themselves, welcoming them to the dinner, and just making them feel at home.

"In the weeks that followed," Fisk adds, "the same

family group helped the new family get settled in the community and also led them to the Lord. Now they are active in a family group themselves."

Another young man, an alcoholic, shyly entered the church at the invitation of a family group leader. No one knew about his problem until he confessed it one day, saying, "I'm not afraid to tell you this because I know I'm accepted here."

He, too, became a Christian and an active member.

Host Families

The Souderton Mennonite Church of Souderton, Pennsylvania, features a similar service for its visitors, but on a slightly smaller scale.

Two families are selected by a team leader to be greeters for the entire month. One family covers each door (front and rear) of the church, and they write down the names of visitors.

These names are then given to the morning ushers, who also extend a welcoming hand to the new folks. While they are doing this, they tell the people that a host family would like to have them over for Sunday dinner. Then after the service the usher introduces the visitors to the day's host family.

"The host family is contacted during the previous week," says program coordinator Ethel Clemmer. "They are instructed to prepare a meal on Sunday for approximately ten extra people."

In the program's first two years, no family had more than ten people to entertain. And on days when there are less than ten visitors in the morning service, the host family is encouraged to invite regular church members to its dinner.

One week, for instance, six visitors came to church. A family of four had recently joined the church, but they didn't know many people yet. So the host family invited all ten people to their dinner and, in Clemmer's words, "It worked out perfectly."

Pastor Glenn Egli adds, "For some reason we often have two families joining the host family for dinner. It just seems to work out that way.

"If we would have too many visitors in the church," says Egli, "one or two of our families would take some new people out to a restaurant for dinner."

First-Timers Welcome, Second-Timers More So

Dennis Marquardt appreciates first-time visitors in the church, but it's the *second*-timers who get the red-carpet treatment.

"We try to make first-timers feel welcome," says Marquardt, pastor of the Assembly of God Christian Center near Vergennes, Vermont. "We send them a letter the next week with information about the church. But so many people will come one time just out of curiosity or because they're passing through that we feel it's wasted energy to follow up each of them."

As soon as visitors come a second time, however, the church springs into action. One of the three elders invites them over for a meal that week.

"When a person comes a second time, that shows a definite interest," says Marquardt.

"We planted this church with nine people 4½ years ago, and we knew the best evangelism was personal, not a program. We've had this treatment for second-timers from the beginning. Now as people have been saved and brought into the church, they just assume this hospitality is what every church is supposed to do. Our members are taking the initiative to invite newcomers over."

The only problem is that as the church has grown to

more than 100 on Sunday morning, keeping up with all the second-timers is more difficult.

So recently, the previously informal routine was given a bit of structure. Bevie Jo Marquardt, Dennis's wife, was elected to oversee the hospitality and make sure no one is overlooked.

"We feel our energy needs to be spent on people with a hunger and thirst for what the church can provide," says Marquardt. "This approach has worked for us."

Visitors with a Smile

When Montford L. Neal came to Meadowlawn Church of God in Middletown, Ohio, back in 1978, Tuesday night visitation drew no more than about eight faithful workers. Switching to Saturday morning didn't help; "people didn't want to give up that block of time and be away from their families," the pastor explains.

Today, lay visitation at Meadowlawn is running smoothly without fatigue or burnout, thanks to Pastor Neal's "Shepherd's Staff" concept. "We set up seven visitation teams of three to five members each. The unique thing is that each team works one week and then has the next six off."

How busy is a team during its active week? "They probably make 10 to 15 personal calls among them, stopping to see visitors from the previous Sunday, shut-ins, absentees, hospital patients, and other names submitted by the congregation. They'll also make some phone calls and send some cards — whatever's appropriate. They don't have to do their work on any given night; they plan their own schedule, whenever it's most convenient for them to do it. The team captain is responsible to fill out records and to report to the overall visitation coordinator on what's been accomplished.

"But then — that's all for seven weeks. The team is

'off duty' until its turn comes around again. People who understandably got 'weary in well-doing' week after week in the old system have really turned on to this method." All the teams come together at the end of a visiting cycle (every seventh week) to discuss results, make suggestions, and receive training.

One woman told Pastor Neal, with tears in her eyes, "This is the first time in my life that I've ever gotten involved in talking to people about spiritual things." Lay leaders regularly refer to the Shepherd's Staff program as "one of our stronger points" and "one of the reasons for our steady growth."

Signs of Friendliness

Members of the Church of Christ in the small town of Dardanelle, Arkansas, carry their hospitality beyond smiles and handshakes on Sunday morning.

Nestled in a wooded valley along miles of scenic lake, Dardanelle attracts many vacationers. If they're looking for a friendly church in which to worship, they don't have to look very far.

On scores of front lawns stands a neat sign. White block lettering on a red background proclaims, "THIS FAMILY INVITES YOU to the Dardanelle Church of Christ."

A local lumber dealer, who prefers to remain anonymous, donated everything — lumber, nails, paint, tools, and labor. Members of the congregation only have to pick up a sign and erect it in their yards next to their own tree-shaded streets.

Reported by Ernestine Gravley

Ads for the Mad and the Curious

Church advertisements in the newspapers can do more than print service times, sermon topics, and a photo of a grinning pastor. Two fresh twists used by St. Monica's Parish in Moraga, California, apparently touched a responsive nerve among the unchurched. One ad, which ran twice in the local paper, read:

CATHOLICS
Inactive? Alienated? Retired? If you've parted company with the church over new changes, old rules, a marriage situation, hurt feelings, or any other reason, why not join us for an open meeting. . . .

"Sixty-five people came, some hostile," says Pastor Brian Joyce. "Since I was expecting only 15 or so, I had to play it by ear. On a large sheet of paper, I listed people's replies to the sentence: 'Church goers become inactive because . . .' " Replies ranged from "offensive clergy" to "too little biblical teaching."

Says Joyce: "I was encouraged when 19 of those 65 asked for a personal visit with the pastor and are now attending services again."

A second ad invited the public to a 45-minute guided tour of St. Monica's Church, seeing the sanctuary, confessionals, and sacristy, and hearing an explanation of Catholic worship and tradition. "Everyone is welcome, no charge and no strings attached," the ad read.

"The teaching tour drew 15 people on Sunday afternoon and 18 people on Monday night," Joyce says. "There was a good exchange, fellowship, and seven unchurched persons joined us.

"These ads have helped us contact people we otherwise would have missed."

Taking the Fear Out of Visitation

"Visitation" scares a lot of people. But it doesn't have to, as Beaver Dam Baptist Church in Kentucky discovered.

"When people think of visitation, they imagine an evangelistic, soul-winning visit," says Michael McCool, minister of education and youth. "Many people fear having to present their testimony to strangers."

But there are, he notes, other kinds of visitation: the awareness visit, the counseling visit, the redemptive visit, the fellowship visit, and the ministry visit.

"Our staff analyzed the various visitation needs we had," says McCool. "To the list above, we added prospect visitation, contact with those regularly absent, and hospital and homebound visits."

What the church has done is to specify one day each week as Visitation Day. Then they set up a "Visitation Board," a bulletin board divided up by the different visits that need to be made.

Under each category, thumbtacked cards give the name, address, and other pertinent information about the person or family. On Visitation Day, people come by the church from 9 A.M. to 7 P.M., take names off the board, and pick up written material to leave with those they visit.

"We've had good success with our board," says McCool. "We've found people who are good at making hospital visits, people who are gifted at making 'cold' prospect visits, and those who are good at redeeming chronic absentees.

"The Visitation Board removes some of the fear. People are better able to use the abilities God has given them. What often happens is that visits become evangelistic even though they don't start that way."

Unlocking Door-to-Door Success

Before you write off door-to-door calling as intrusive or too scary, consider the experience of Brookville Baptist Church in Holbrook, Massachusetts. For the past seven summers they've run a town-wide program that has made friends, not enemies, and has brought new people into the church.

Two keys are:

• Sending an advance letter to the home that says someone will be stopping by with a complimentary copy of one of the four gospels. "You must tell people ahead of time what is expected of them," says Pastor James Eubanks, who spent seven years in business before entering this pastorate. "A letter makes all the difference. Instead of being surprised or affronted, people welcome this gift."

• Taking advantage of hot weather (especially in New England, where air conditioning is less than universal). "For years our best evangelism has been during the summer," says Eubanks. "People are more receptive. They're out on their porches or the lawn, more willing to talk. The hotter the better."

Inviting children to Vacation Bible School is especially fruitful, according to the Brookville callers. "When it's hot, people want to give you their kids for a couple of hours — even atheists," says the pastor.

"We have to bring direct action back into the church. We have to go public with the gospel." Door-to-door calling, apparently, is one such method that isn't worn out yet.

Adapted from New England Church Life

After the Field Survey

Once you go to the work of an every-house survey, how do you keep it current so you won't have to do it all again in three years?

LeRoy A. Peterson, while pastor of the Baptist church in Ashport, Tennessee, made sure his data stayed reliable by asking each deacon to watch over a zone and bring a monthly update. "We mapped out what we considered to be our church field — about 50 square miles of rural area there along the Mississippi River," says Peterson, who now teaches at a Baptist school in Kentucky. "We marked every dwelling on the map, about 200 in all. I did the initial survey myself, stopping at each house to find out names, ages, and church affiliation, if any. That way I got to meet a lot of people, and they got to know me.

"From that point on, the deacons took responsibility for noting who was moving out and moving in. I furnished each one with a map of his territory and the necessary survey cards. Each month he would bring in any changes or new information to the church office. We always stayed up-to-date this way."

A side benefit of the plan, of course, was that the deacons got involved in home visitation and kept in touch with needs in the community.

"We never had to worry about our information being obsolete," says Peterson. "We were always informed about each family in this farming community."

The Quiet Canvass

When Pastor Steven Bunkoff and the Congregational church decided to canvass every home in their small town of Savannah, New York, they printed no brochures or newsletters. They ordered no tracts. They didn't even ring a single doorbell.

All they did was pray.

Street by street, week after week from July through to the end of the year, they asked God to touch the lives of those who lived (or worked) on each of the town's 40 streets. Bunkoff used a red marker to highlight each week's target on a map mounted at the front of the sanctuary. Occasionally he grouped short or sparsely populated streets, so that the entire town was covered in about 25 weeks. Each Sunday morning, he led the congregation in prayer and urged them to continue throughout the week, not naming individuals but only the street.

Did anything happen?

"People began visiting our church, and there was no 'natural' explanation — other than that we prayed," says the pastor. "One Sunday four families from one street came after our week of praying for them. Two of those have continued to attend the church, one becoming very involved."

When Bunkoff first presented the idea to the church board, there was lengthy discussion about whether to have face-to-face calling, too. "We finally decided to go with strictly prayer," Bunkoff says. "I think some of our people were genuinely surprised at the results. They supported the canvass, but they were still amazed when visitors began showing up.

"Actually, we didn't pray that people would necessarily come to our church. We only prayed that God would touch their lives. And he has."

One Is Enough

When it comes to personal evangelism, "people are more likely to commit themselves to a task that appears manageable," says Geoffrey W. Posegate, pastor of two United Methodist churches in the southeast corner of Missouri. Thus, he has devised a one-to-one strategy for Trinity UMC in the county seat town of Bloomfield (pop. 1,600).

In the fall of 1980, planners began by updating a list of prospects — every local person they knew who had no active church affiliation. They easily came up with nearly 40 individuals, couples, or families.

Next, they began matching each prospect with an active member of the church. "We paid a lot of attention to natural bridges of kinship, friendship, similar interests or life-situations, employment, and age," says Posegate. "We didn't just throw names together at random."

Throughout the fall each member was contacted personally and asked to make a commitment for 1981:

- To visit or call the prospect at least once a month
- To be ready to *listen* and watch for opportunities to share what Christ means personally
- To invite the prospect to special church activities.

"In a year's time, we began to see results," Posegate reports. "Eight new members joined the church because of these personal contacts. People began commenting to me cheerfully about the number of 'new faces' in worship. Our Sunday school ran about 12 to 15 percent ahead of a year before."

Do the prospects feel hounded by Trinity people? "We've talked a lot with our members about what we've termed 'overkill,' " the pastor adds. "We've urged the use of discretion; we've said, 'When you go to visit, don't stay forever. If you visit one month, just make a phone call the next. And in every situation, *listen* as much as you talk."

"We've had no resistance so far. In fact, one prospect sent a member a Valentine card with a note that said, 'We appreciate your keeping us informed about what's going on at the church.' "

Are members allowed to give up if prospects are not receptive? Yes. "We stay in close touch, and if a match-up is going nowhere, we'll let it ride for a while, or reassign the member to another person," Posegate explains. Internal communication is aided by a phone-calling pyramid from the pastor to the evangelism chairwoman to five sub-callers, each of whom is in touch with four to seven others. Thus, news and information can move quickly in both directions.

"In our second year, 25 active individuals or couples were making contact. I believe evangelism is most effective on a person-to-person basis, and this is one such method."

A Sign of Life

New babies characteristically let out a cry when they're born, a welcome sign of life. How do spiritual newborns greet their new life?

In Wenatchee, Washington, it's also with their lungs.

Evangelism teams from the Free Methodist church are trained to ask a specific question whenever a person commits himself to Christ: "Who do you know in town that you'd like to tell about this decision right now?" The member guides the new believer to phone a Christian friend on the spot. If he doesn't know one, he calls one of the pastors to explain what he's just done.

"We're convinced the new Christian needs to go public immediately to confirm the decision," says Pastor George Delamarter (since relocated to Salem, Oregon). "We make sure, though, that the person called is someone who understand the significance and supports the decision."

The phone calls are just a small part of the church's active evangelistic thrust.

"About a third of our people" (700 on Sunday morning) "are new Christians," says Delamarter. Almost all of those are a result of the Tuesday night visitation.

Teams of two call on church visitors and people whose names are listed with Welcome Wagon. The initial visit is a casual get-acquainted conversation, but the team asks if the hosts would be interested in a brief Bible study on how a person can get to heaven. If the response is positive, a follow-up session is scheduled in their home the next week.

"Of the people who have gone through the Bible study, 80 percent have accepted Christ," says Delamarter. "That's 200 people in the last year, and 35 percent of those have joined the church."

A Milestone to Share

To make water baptism a public witness to as many as possible, one West Coast church provides invitations for each candidate to mail out. Friends, relatives, and associates at work receive a printed card:

We invite you to join us
for a celebration of
Christian joy
as
[Name]
becomes obedient to the Lord through
Christian baptism
on
[Date]
at
Valley Christian Church
811 Marylin Ave.
Livermore, CA 94550
10:45 a.m.

"We've used these for more than a year now," says Pastor Larry Trummel, "and people have been excited about the number of friends attending. One man was responsible for 30 individuals all by himself the morning he was baptized."

Outreach with a Feminine Touch

Women's midweek groups, traditionally for fellowship, are in some places developing evangelistic thrusts as well. Two examples from the Northwest:

At Christian Life Assembly in Langley, British Columbia, "Women Alive" is a two-hour program on Thursday mornings.

● The first hour is strictly an exercise class, led by a trained fitness instructor.

● The second hour offers 12-week electives on a wide range of topics: dieting, Bible book studies, "The Creative Woman," "The Mid-Life Crisis," "How to Really Love Your Child," "Learning to Talk with God."

When Marilyn Lebeck, the senior pastor's wife, began the program four years ago, 40 women attended. Last year, Women Alive averaged 140, many of them from outside the congregation. A young mother named Elsie Sharp is typical: "I was invited by a friend," she says. "I'd only gone to Sunday school briefly as a child and hadn't been in church since. But here they explained the basics of Christianity, and after a few weeks, I accepted Christ into my life at home in my bedroom." She's now a regular attender of Christian Life Assembly.

Name tags are used by everyone to encourage friendships. Nursery and toddler care is provided each week. Textbooks are sold for some of the courses, which run in three terms: September to early December, January to March, and mid-April to June.

The teachers, all women of the church, use the first-hour exercise time to meet for prayer, problem solving, and planning. "This program has developed leadership among our women and provided many ministry opportunities," says David Lim, associate pastor. "The low-key, esteem-building approach has won a good number of families to the Lord and the church."

Thursdays are also outreach days in Tacoma, Washington, when First Covenant Church women minister to young wives of soldiers at Fort Lewis.

"Circles of Love" amounts to a two-hour mother's workshop, with presentations on everything from health and nutrition to budgeting and puppetry. Crafts are also a favorite with the 15 or so who attend.

"Most of them are 17 to 22 years old, far from home, trying to make it on military pay with one or more children," says Pastor Robert Bergquist. "For some, it's their only chance of the week to get out of the apartment."

Sharon Romero and Susan Day, who lead the ministry, find lots of chances for counseling and one-to-one witness. "The friendships have become very deep," says Day, "and personal problems come to the surface readily. We've had times when gals have just broken down and cried in our arms because of various frustrations."

The Thursday workshop is held in a Presbyterian church near the base, while First Covenant's Christian education budget covers all costs for crafts and other supplies. As in Langley, child care is considered a must.

The ripple effect of "Circle of Love" has reached as far as the chaplains, who are now referring young wives who seem to need a support base. A Monday Bible study has also sprung up in a home.

Ready-made Audiences

Two different churches have found dramatic response to the idea of taking Sunday school where unchurched children are already clustered. Reports from Kentucky and Oklahoma:

If Dad is in prison, what does a child do on visitation days after the initial greetings are over? Mom has a list of things to discuss, and the hours waiting around a penitentiary can get long.

That's why the people of LaGrange Christian Church began classes on Saturday and Sunday afternoons at Roederer Farm Center, one of three penal institutions in their small town east of Louisville. "Every week, the kids are just sitting out in the hall, waiting for us to show up," says William McConnell, minister. "Saturdays draw around 15, Sundays 20 or more. We start at 1:30 on both days and go for an hour or longer."

One problem, of course, is that the population keeps changing as fathers are paroled (Roederer is a minimum-security facility, often an inmate's last stop before release). Another challenge is that the age range can run from three-year-olds to teenagers. "But the older kids help the younger ones at craft time," says teacher Mary Ann Perry, "and we get along fine. One 16-year-old always says, 'My mom made me come' — but there's a big grin on his face when he says it. He enjoys helping the little ones cut and paste."

The Perry daughter, 12, and a girlfriend from the church are the songleaders, while McConnell plays guitar. The prison class uses the same curriculum as the church, so each child leaves with something made by hand. "At Christmastime, we made ornaments for the tree in the prison chapel," says Perry. The result: some fathers darkened the chapel door for the first time of their stay.

"Our main emphasis," says the teacher, "is on Jesus' love for each of them. We're showing what love is all about."

When Mike Dumler came to serve the Christian church in Mulhall, Oklahoma, he couldn't help noticing the army of children — many from non-Christian homes — streaming into the school across the street each morning. How could he reach them for Christ?

Then, after a successful Vacation Bible School in 1981, the staff raised an excellent question: "Why stop now?" That fall the church began what amounts to a second Sunday school, only it's on Tuesday afternoons the instant school lets out.

"We call our outreach TABS (Tuesday Afternoon Bible School)," says Dumler. "A week after the fall term began, I sent a letter to the parents of every elementary child announcing our program and urging them to 'keep TABS on your kids.' This generated a lot of inquiries and support. We found out parents in this town *want* their children to receive Bible teaching.

"On our launching day, our director, Cheryl Major, and I got permission to go into every classroom at the end of the day and invite the children to 'come right across the street for Bible classes.' TABS quickly became the popular thing to do after school, so that now we're drawing 70 children each week — half the school's enrollment."

The hour begins with an after-school snack; workers arrive 30-60 minutes early to have the goodies waiting on the tables when the children race in. Then the three age-graded classes begin, using Standard's New Life curriculum, which has an awards system to motivate kids who could just as easily be on the playground. Scripture memorization is prominent, along with Bible stories, worship, and crafts.

There's also a nursery to accommodate the preschoolers of those who teach.

The minister lists several benefits so far:

- "A number of the Tuesday children have started coming on Sunday morning as well.

- "Many of our members who had no ministry in the church are now very active in TABS.

- "Seventy hearts and minds in their most formative years are hearing the Word of God and memorizing it."

THE LEAST OF THESE MY NEIGHBORS

by Don Baker, pastor, Hinson Memorial Baptist Church, Portland, Oregon

In January, 1982, I had just finished preaching from Hebrews 12 on "How to Cope in a Crisis" when a young mother met me in the hallway with tears in her eyes.

"Oh, Pastor, thank you," she said. "You'll never know how much God is using these messages in our lives. We have lost our business, our home, our car, and we just don't know what's next. I don't know what we'd do without your encouragement."

As I walked away, I was smitten. *Encouragement,* I thought. *She needs more than encouragement. She needs help, and she needs it now.*

I called the staff, the deacons, and the deaconesses together, and we began a program we later called "Hinson's Helping Ministry." It was primarily for Hinson members.

We announced a special meeting for all the unemployed and underemployed in the church on Wednesday evening. People from 60 households responded. The enormity of the problem was frightening.

We began uncovering needs and seeking out resources, supervised completely by the members of the church. We solicited food, freezers, refrigerators, clothing, and money from the congregation in order to begin an immediate assistance program.

I met with the unemployed each Wednesday night to pray and share together, and then a specialist provided counsel in areas such as:

- Finding jobs when they're scarce
- Preparing résumés
- Food shopping on a low income
- Working with creditors
- Finding available money
- What medical assistance is available
- Government assistance programs

In these meetings we distributed cash for food and emergency needs and made arrangements for clothing and aid in job hunting.

Within 90 days we had located most of the "hurting" and had disbursed over $15,000, distributed food to 379 families and clothing to nearly 200 more families, collected more than 15 tons of food and filled two houses with usable clothing. Through people within the church, we had placed 89 persons in full-time or part-time jobs. In the month of March alone, 3,414 meals were served through our Loaves and Fishes (meals-on-wheels) program.

But people outside the church were hurting, too.

Our state had 161,000 unemployed, with an estimated 25,000 more who had quit looking and were not on unemployment rolls. Meanwhile, $350 million had been chopped from social service programs in Oregon.

In the Buckman and Sunnyside neighborhoods surrounding our church, 70 percent of the population received less than Portland's median income.

We discovered 1,440 households were earning less than $10,000 per year, and 562 households were living on less than $5,000 per year.

For over a year the staff had been concerned with a double objective: First, to penetrate a somewhat hostile community. Second, to mobilize more members of the Hinson family.

Suddenly we realized we had the catalyst: the recession.

With a neighborhood population of 14,000, however, we knew our church didn't have the resources to make a serious impact. Any attempt at significant ministry to neigbors would be futile.

So we began dreaming big, crossing denominational barriers. Soon we'd gathered an organization of 14 churches with 8,000 worshipers and secured the cooperation of available social agencies. We enlisted members of the neighborhood associations and established a ministry we called Reach-Out.

The uniqueness of Reach-Out is that, unlike other agencies, we deal in services — not goods.

Others distribute food, clothing, and funds, but none is organized to put skilled people together with those who have needs but not funds.

Each church solicited volunteers who would be willing to assist a neighbor in need. We listed more than 30 categories, from plumbing and auto repairs to baby-sitting and grocery shopping. Nearly 1,000 church people responded.

The churches pooled their financial resources and hired a young couple as coordinators. Louis Bencze, an underemployed commercial photographer, and his wife, Rebecca, an unemployed nurse, began filing the names of the volunteers according to skills, times available, church membership, and location. Then they secured a telephone number, 234-6333 (234-NEED).

After defining the geographic area we could reach, 10,000 handbills were distributed — one to each Buckman and Sunnyside household. We also bought newspaper and television advertising.

Our presentation was simple:

DO YOU HAVE A NEED? CALL 234-NEED
Your neighbors are now organized and available to provide services free of charge if you're unemployed or can't afford them — everything from carpentry to baby-sitting.

We decided each request would be screened by a brief visit from the coordinators before a volunteer would be dispatched.

Reach-Out Churches

These 14 churches are working together in Portland's
Buckman and Sunnyside neighborhoods.

Centenary-Wilbur Methodist Church
Colonial Heights United Presbyterian Church
Community Bible Fellowship Church
Epworth United Methodist Church
Grace and Truth Pentecostal Church
Hinson Memorial Baptist Church
Laurelhurst Bible Church
Mennonite Church of Portland
Neighborhood Church
Open Door Fellowship Church
Portland Foursquare Church
Portland Temple Wings of Healing
St. Francis of Assisi Catholic Church
Sunnyside United Methodist Church

The newly installed telephone began to ring imediately, 38 calls the first day.

One woman asked if someone would repair her electric heater. She couldn't afford to call an electrician. The Benczes called an electrician from one of the local churches. Within a few hours the heater was fixed.

A three-alarm fire hit a neighborhood apartment, causing extensive damage. Within hours the coordinators were in the building, distributing the Reach-Out number and advising the management that local churches had people available to help.

An 81-year-old blind lady called and asked for someone to help her write letters.

We're cautious about proselytizing. Nevertheless, all churches recognize it as pre-evangelism, breaking down walls between Christian and non-Christian.

Meanwhile, Hinson Memorial continues to give away necessities. I stood in our Amos House recently as clothing was being distributed and rejoiced with a young man and his family who had just prayed to receive Christ. He couldn't believe that churches could care so much.

Our dreams are being realized: the neighborhood is being penetrated, local-church members are being mobilized, 14 community churches have found a way to cooperate without compromise, political differences are being ignored, the needy are being helped, Christ is becoming visible through his church, and people are falling in love with him.

For us the recession is proving to be an occasion for what may be the church's finest hour — not falling into a social gospel, but rising to use social needs as an occasion for the gospel to become visible.

The Outsiders' Inn

A four-room cottage First Baptist Church of Ft. Walton Beach, Florida, acquired when it bought property next door is being put to good use until the day it's torn down for church expansion. The little house is offered free to families coming to visit inmates at nearby Eglin Federal Prison Camp.

"By the time these women and their children make a long trip to see Dad, there certainly isn't money left over for a motel," explains Pastor James L. Monroe. "So for the last five years or so, we've made the cottage available as part of our overall ministry out at Eglin." (The church also does Sunday school, a Tuesday night Bible class, and special events in conjunction with Prison Fellowship.)

Families hear about the lodging through inmates or the prison chaplain. Some stay just a weekend, other for several weeks. Maintenance is handled by the church custodian, while the missions committee oversees and sets policy.

Guests don't usually attend Sunday morning worship at the church, since they're out at the prison for visiting hours. But some come on Sunday nights or to the midweek potluck; children and teens join the church's various youth activities.

The only problem Monroe remembers was one man who, upon release, stayed in the house a few days and used the address to charge merchandise at local stores before slipping away. "But on the other hand," says the pastor, "another family stayed there for an extended time, and when the dad got out, they decided to settle here in town. That man is now a deacon in our church."

A Church Has Done the Walking

What can a church do for new residents that will help them immediately? The Troy (Illinois) United Methodist Church has created a simple tool to meet a practical need.

"We're in a fast-growing community near Scott Air Force Base," says Pastor Edward Weston. "One evening, talking with several military people new to town, I asked what kinds of needs they had right now. One lady said it sure would be handy to have all the important phone numbers on one sheet."

So church members developed an information sheet on a piece of legal-size paper. One side contains phone numbers for:

- Schools
- Weather and road conditions
- Police and fire
- Poison control center
- Hospitals
- Utilities
- Key city agencies (driver's license, vehicle sticker, voter information)
- Frequently called Scott AFB facilites (commissary, base exchange, credit union)

The other side offers a brief description of Troy and the services and activities available. "For additional information and assistance," the church prints its name, logo, address, and phone number at the bottom.

Weston hands out the sheets when he calls on newcomers, and several realtors in town distribute them to prospective home buyers.

"I can't say we've gotten any new members as a result of this sheet," says Weston. "But people have been grateful. Lots of people post it right next to the phone."

Thanks, Officer

The sight of a policeman walking toward you sometimes causes heart palpitations. But the night the police invaded Bible Temple in Portland, Oregon, it was a heart-warming, not a heart-thumping, occasion.

The event was a "Law Enforcement Appreciation Banquet." Because the nature of police work puts such stress on family life, and the demanding schedule makes regular church involvement difficult, Bible Temple and cosponsoring Portland churches invited over 1,800 city police, sheriff's deputies, state troopers, and FBI officers to what has become an annual fete.

For the past several years, more than 400 officers and wives have attended the free first-class banquet featuring prime rib and cheesecake served by candlelight. Church members dressed in formal black and white wait on the tables. Afterward, everyone moves to the church sanctuary for a program of patriotic, country-western, and black gospel music, comedy, and testimonies of appreciation.

At the 1982 event, Don Baker, pastor of Portland's Hinson Memorial Baptist Church, was the main speaker. Baker, who has spent time riding in squad cars and even received a letter of commendation for assisting an officer during a street fight, "was able to experientially express appreciation for the commitment of the officers," says B. J. Johnston, Bible Temple's assistant pastor.

"In addition, his vivid, real-life illustration of a man falling five stories to his death because he refused to accept a helping hand drove home the fact that God's helping hand is needed by everyone, even law enforcement officers.

"But the officers weren't preached to," says Johnston. "Our purpose was to encourage a group that's too rarely appreciated, to assure them of church support."

"I thought it was pretty neat," says Oregon City police officer Harry Swofford. "There's so much negative input to us. It's nice to receive something without strings attached. They didn't push Christianity on anyone. The pastors who spoke were just themselves."

The idea arose when a few officers attending Bible Temple told Pastor Dick Iverson how morale had dropped as a result of bad publicity. The Portland police department had been criticized for abuses by narcotics officers and an opossum-dumping incident by North Precinct officers. Iverson suggested a pastors' group he belonged to would be interested in helping out.

With the help of Portland Police Chaplain Ed Stelle and other active and retired officers, the first banquet was held in November, 1981. The next year, 39 churches plus Multnomah School of the Bible and Western Conservative Baptist Seminary supported the banquet. Not counting the volunteer labor, the effort cost around $1,800.

The banquet has succeeded in breaking down some barriers.

"Many of the men were hesitant to come because it was held in a church," says Johnston. "But they ended up feeling comfortable. One believing wife wrote us to say her unsaved husband had been impressed with Bible Temple. She wrote: 'He even said he would enjoy visiting there with me one evening!' "
Reported by Julia Duin

A Video Game with Redeeming Value

If a church wants to minister at a county fair, how can it attract passersby tastefully?

One answer: Use a computer game. "Maze to Heaven" was the name of the program Jeff Glover, a high school junior, wrote for the booth run by Trade Lake Baptist Church, Frederic, Wisconsin. Using multiple-choice questions supplied by his pastor, Glover created a little man who traveled down a road and faced a question about salvation at each intersection. If the player gave the correct answer, the character on the screen made progress. An incorrect answer meant running down a dead end.

"We drew a lot of traffic during the three days of the fair," says Pastor Dale Cope. "It was interesting to watch people's expressions as they found out what the Bible really said." Opportunities for personal witness came naturally as Trade Lake members at the booth struck up conversations with game players.

"This project became an enjoyable and effective way to share the Good News with a computer-curious culture," reports the pastor.

Congregation of the Unchurched

When Keith Maxwell was pastoring in Salem, Oregon, he ministered not only to the Englewood United Methodist Church but also to a group of unchurched friends — "The Viking IV Clientele."

"I adopted them as my congregation in the world," says Maxwell, who now has moved to a church in Portland. "They were state employees, bank tellers, contractors, and retirees. They ranged in age from 25 to 75. The only thing they had in common was breakfast."

Each morning they gathered at the Viking IV Restaurant, a "mom and pop" cafe that serves Norwegian entrees.

"In the cafe — my chapel, if you please — two counters face each other with tables for four in between," says Maxwell. "It's the kind of place where if you order 'one pancake,' you get two."

About three mornings a week, Maxwell would stop in for coffee, joining the regulars at the counter near the kitchen.

"They called it 'The Bench' because over the counter we'd pass our blue- and white-collar judgments on all sorts of local, national, and world problems," says Maxwell.

The Clientele evolved into Maxwell's informal congregation.

"I offered opinions on the death penalty and drives for tax reform. But I also listened to stories of heartache and heartbreak, counseled those in the pain of divorce, and comforted those mourning the loss of a spouse. I put my arm on the shoulder of an alcoholic who lost his wife and legal practice, and I gave hope to a terminally ill veteran."

Because he was the only pastor many of these people had known, Maxwell was asked to officiate at funeral services, visit sick and dying loved ones, and counsel and perform weddings for sons and daughters.

"These people need pastoral ministry," says Maxwell. "I believe Jesus would be in the Viking IV, even as he went to Zacchaeus's home. The witness of Christ can be made casually but effectively by discussing issues, sharing needs, and extending personal friendship."

THE MISSION FIELD CAME TO US

by Robert V. Bergquist, pastor, First Covenant Church, Tacoma, Washington

We had never had a baptismal service quite like the one that New Year's Eve. For one thing, my associate and I had never worked so hard to be ready to pronounce the candidates' names accurately. "Dave Smith" posed no problem, but "Tem Sayavong," "Somphong Sonesouphab," and "Pheng Phongsa" called for our utmost in concentration.

The other uniqueness on this night was that First Covenant was once again bilingual. In the same congregation where our Scandinavian forebears mingled Swedish and English, seven of the nine new believers now gave their testimonies in Laotian, with translation. There were tears of joy as the sons and daughters of immigrants past welcomed these latest refugees into the fellowship of Christ's church.

How did all this happen? We had no grand expectations in the beginning; we simply affirmed the vision of two people in our church in early 1980 that we open our arms to one of the world's homeless families. Our denomination was offering financial assistance to any church that would take this step, and so in May, "our family" arrived.

Vanhsy Phommavongsay turned out to be a former military officer with good English skills. He, his wife, and two children moved in with the Holdych family and began learning about American life and culture. Although they seemed uninterested in their hosts' Christian faith, they appreciated the kindness and help the Holdychs extended.

Our first ministry, therefore, took the form of simple *caring*. As it turned out, other Laotians new in the city gravitated toward Vanhsy for guidance. "Call the refugee committee at this church," he kept saying. "They'll help you any way they can." When the Bounsong family arrived during the summer, he noticed a Bible among their possessions. "You will probably want to go to their meetings," Vanhsy added, "since you have the same book."

Committee members Bill and Nancy Siems brought the new family to church in September, and others began to reach out to these Southeast Asian guests. John and Carol Pearson, who both work in special education, entertained them more than once, while Carol Tyler, a teacher of English as a second language, started to go to their home to tutor.

When Thongsa Buonsong lay seriously ill for several days, Carol kept a vigil by her hospital bed. There was a touching moment when Thongsa awoke to find her friend still there; she could have no doubt she was truly cared for. Carol also prayed and encouraged the woman and her husband through a time of marital stress and saw the relationship restored.

To our caring we added *teaching*. In February of 1981, we started a Laotian Sunday school class. It became obvious that the Laotian men would respond much better to a male teacher. So Steve Weber, a recent college graduate with a great interest in missions, taught the class, helped by a young Laotian interpreter. The two worked so closely that in time the young refugee also took the name Stephen.

Meanwhile, Frank Wallin, a retired missionary to India, took charge of getting the furniture, clothing, bedding, and other articles donated by the congregation to those who needed them. He also taxied persons to the welfare office, doctor, and dentist. The Vacation Bible School children collected hundreds of helpful items, and the message continued to spread that the people of the church cared.

But our spiritual breakthrough didn't come until last August, more than a year into the outreach. We had been praying that this growing group in our midst might come to salvation. That prayer began to be answered when a couple who had been attending the class opened their hearts to Jesus after a visit with some Laotian Christians north of Tacoma. Tem, the husband, was so overjoyed that he asked continually to tell the class about his spiritual birth. Through his testimony, combined with Steve's lessons that called for decision, a great number turned from Buddhism to follow Christ.

And when three-week-old David Phongsa was given the role of baby Jesus in the Christmas program, it was obvious that the Savior was not just an American.

On a typical Sunday, John Pearson now brings 45 Laotians on the church bus, and another 30 or so come by other means. They constitute more than 10 percent of the congregation; there is no doubt they are an integral part of the church. In an unsettled time in their lives, they have found friends who truly love and give of themselves, because of Jesus. And they are now sharing with their friends the good news of what they have found.

The members of First Covenant, on the other hand, are dealing with the realities of our continuing responsibilities. Sunday school teachers must stretch as they work with children from two cultures. We've budgeted 12 hours of English classes each week to enable faster integration into American life. George Nelson, our minister of Christian education, is carefully monitoring what the proposed government cutbacks will mean to the refugee community. We may face a call for greater aid in the future.

But we are glad nevertheless to have been drawn into this kind of ministry. Without ever stepping onto a jetliner, we have been plunged into cross-cultural missionary work. Which group has been the beneficiary? Clearly, both of us.

A MINISTRY WE DIDN'T THINK WE WANTED

by Celeste S. McFarland, Grace Presbyterian Church,
Lexington, Virginia

Nobody said so aloud, but we knew he wasn't a "normal" visitor, here to try out the church after buying a house in the neighborhood. Dressed in black pants and jacket with an open-collared white shirt, he was sitting quietly on a folding chair when the first regulars arrived for Sunday school.

When offered a handshake, he seemed hesitant, embarrassed, and his eyes darted quickly away. Nor did he really speak; his words were mumbled. When he left that day, no one could say what his name was.

Wednesday night prayer meeting came, and there he was again. When you sat in a circle, you noticed his feet. So small. Shiny, orthopedic shoes covered the feet of a boy, not the man with a lined face dressed again in black and white. And those eyes. He wasn't trying to look away from people — he was trying to look *at* them. His eyes were so crossed he could not make them look straight at you. Concentrated listening to his garbled speech revealed that his name was Jackie and that he was "at the hotel across the street."

Our small university town is inhabited with tweedy, professorial types, seasoned with an occasional outright eccentric. But none like Jackie. "At the hotel across the street" explained why this less-than-preppy type had walked into our church. Deinstitutionalization was on our block. The owners of the hotel, the Royal Hosts Inn, had been granted a license to operate an adult home — a residence for people from institutions who have been judged able to function in society with a little help. At the Royal Hosts, they would be responsible for their own personal needs, but the staff would provide meals.

When summer arrived, so did our church's custom of backyard picnicking on Wednesdays. Jackie was a regular by this time, and he was always at the church — early — waiting for a ride. But he was not alone. There was Ed — tall, with slicked-back red hair. Then there was Nina, her haunting look accentuated with eye make-up and her Jehovah's Witness Bible tucked under her arm. We made more food to feed them.

Did anyone see the outline of God's providence and where he was leading our congregation? Probably not.

Grace Church is a growing church that looks forward to welcoming newcomers. But frankly, we didn't expect this kind of infusion. These people were different, and we had to adjust. For example, people with adult bodies began vying with the children to collect the Sunday school offering. Class responses might have nothing to do with the lesson. Bibles were shoved at neighbors — and even the pastor — for help in finding a just-announced Scripture. And there was the day a young fellow interrupted the sermon by graphically announcing his intention to go to the bathroom.

While the unpredictable was becoming commonplace, what was the attitude of the congregation?

One member says candidly, "I had no problem with them coming to the church as long as I had no dealings with them. In fact, I felt smug about the church 'letting' them come."

We knew we not only had to "let" these people come, but we had a responsibility toward these troubled creations of God. But what? No one in our congregation of less than 100 members had any formal training, so we felt our way.

We became accustomed to speech impediments. We learned how to communicate with hugs and waves and nods.

We gave a birthday party for Carter, who was always prais-
ing God "for my birthday this week." The problem was, we
gave the party in October and later heard from the hotel
managers that his birthday was in January.

The first organized effort for our Royal Hosts "folks," as
they were called, began with Bob and Cindy Withrow. "We
began to have them in our home and discovered a small
ministry there," says Bob. "We thought it would be good for
them to be away from the Royal Hosts and spend time in
church members' homes, so we decided to take one or two of
them each week and go to someone's home for a meal."

Gib and Debbie Edson were one couple who opened
their home. "We never knew they would need help with a
meal, or that they wouldn't know what to do with a knife
or fork," says Debbie. "And conversation could sometimes get
irrational. Once when a guest was telling stories about his
family, we couldn't tell if he was talking about his sister or his
cat! Having the other couple there certainly helped to ease
the difficulty."

By the summer of 1982 the church had a reputation in
town. Other churches, perhaps with a sigh of relief, praised us
for our efforts and perseverance. Non-Christians declared
that Grace Church was "the way things ought to be." Some of
the Royal Hosts residents had joined the church and
entered various ministries, bringing some personal difficulties
and unpredictability. We learned to make some rules such
as "only one dessert, not a bowlful" and "you have to be able
to read to join the choir."

But still our hearts needed more softening, and more
education.

Sam Calhoun, a church officer, found that the summer of
1982 radically changed his attitudes. Several events set the
process in motion. First, one of the residents who had
joined the church got in trouble with the law, and Calhoun, a
law professor, was asked to help.

"I actually had to spend time with him, the better part of

two days, in fact. I found myself out in the world with him, and I began to see his sense of humor and to relate to him as a person."

Then there was the sermon from a visiting minister who didn't even know about the Royal Hosts. "The text was Romans 3:9," Calhoun recalls, "where Old Testament passages are repeated showing just how we look without Christ. Sure, the Royal Hosts people are unattractive, but so am I without Christ. The church's calling was clear. If we weren't going to respond in a true Christlike manner, well, we had just better close our doors. And I knew I had to get in line.

"Shortly after that, Bob Withrow gave a talk that tied together Matthew 25:40 and Isaiah 53 to show us our responsibility as a church. Christ was the suffering servant, and there was no beauty in him. He was despised. The Royal Hosts houses society's despised people. When we love despised people, we love Christ."

Our low-key, feel-our-way approach was working so far, but the Spirit was moving in us. More was needed, a more organized ministry. Yes, they were welcome; yes, some had made confessions of faith and joined the church; and yes, the management of the hotel would call on us for help occasionally. But we had to go beyond mending clothes and taking them to dinner.

After discussing several options, the elders decided to implement a Bible study program for mentally impaired people published by the Christian Reformed Church. We would host a Friendship Class, as the series is known, and the nucleus of tutors would come from our congregation. We held a meeting for the public and presented the idea. David, Jewish and a victim of cerebral palsy, had become a Christian and joined the church. He told his story and received a round of applause. The class began.

As one member has said, "We seem to move in spurts in this situation. We make a big move, then we sit for a while."

Where we will be in six months or a year we don't know.

But we do know that these people are part of us. Yes, visitors come to the church, feel uncomfortable, and don't come again, but we have been enriched by the Royal Hosts folks in a way that never would have been possible with "normal" people.

Robbie communicates with grunts — exuberant grunts but generally unintelligible. Often at prayer time he mumbles in a prayerful tone. Others let him mumble until he finishes. But once someone did listen. Robbie was not unintelligible. He was repeating over and over, "Jesus loves me, Jesus loves me. . . ."

Hurt, anger, and rage had Carter shaking when he arrived unexpectedly to see the pastor. Someone had hurt him, and he wanted to talk about it. After a short talk the pastor said, "Carter, let's pray and ask the Holy Spirit to help you." Upon the finish of the prayer, Carter immediately held out his hands toward the pastor and said, grinning broadly, "Look, Fred, the Holy Spirit made me stop shaking!"

The simple faith of children in adult bodies is demonstrated to us every day. But the same adult-sized people can also be self-centered, obnoxious, rude — and probably won't change. God knows we need these people, for they show outwardly what we all are inwardly.

Perhaps someday the vision of one member will be a reality, and the entire Royal Hosts operation will be a ministry of our church. But for now we must do what we can. Our doors are open. With God's help, we are living with these people and loving them. And in return, God is loving us through them.

What Churches Can Do

How can the church help integrate the handicapped into society? It's wise to start simple. Offer what you think you can offer.

What about singing? Singing can get attention and capture the most repressed patient, pulling strings from way back. Holding a songbook or teaching a song can be the ideal means for picking up a relationship. And songs with motions benefit not only the spirit but the body.

Including these troubled people in your church's prayer time gives them an opportunity to express caring for others. Feelings can be triggered by prayer that never would surface in traditional therapy.

A church definitely should take advantage of the "gate-keepers," those who look after the deinstitutionalized. In addition to clinic personnel, gatekeepers include operators of senior citizen programs, adult home operators, and managers of sheltered workshops. Offer help; ask for help!

Clinics can give training, and there's a big pay-off in that training. Clinic personnel are so tied up with paperwork and basic mental health that it's often difficult to offer other help to clients. A trained layperson often can do a better job than a professional.

We've learned that a few rules don't hurt. Such rules needn't take the form of "Do this, this, and this, or you can't come to church," but gentle reminders of what behavior is and isn't appropriate can help keep relationships smooth and even guard the safety of the adult home residents. For instance, we had to make a rule that the adult home people not come to church until just before the beginning of the services. They were coming as much as an hour early, and one morning the pastor found a group of them huddled together outside the door — the temperature was five degrees!

It is important to remember that these people want to be treated as normally as possible. Normal people do not run thundering down the aisle in the middle of a service to go to the bathroom. If you have to go, you have to go, but you leave quietly, and you return quietly.

Rarely have we had any contact with the families of the Royal Hosts residents. Often families have cut ties with the troubled, handicapped person, but in cases where there is contact, you can help the resident write letters or help the family members when they come to visit.

No doubt the question of church membership will arise. Of course, this is a situation that must be handled on an individual basis. Some Royal Hosts residents came to us with a basic knowledge of Christianity. They knew that Jesus died for their sins and that the Holy Spirit was in their hearts. Some learned the principles at Grace Church. In either case, they demonstrated to the pastor that they could not only say these things but they also had a desire to let Jesus make a difference in the way they live. Sure they slip, but so do we.

Are there legal liabilities? Not really. The same liabilities exist as in any helping situation. But common sense should tell you not to put a handicapped person in a situation he can't handle. For instance, if you take someone camping, keep an eye out for him as you would a child.

Helping the handicapped can be seen by the church as a threat to its existence or as an opportunity for service, to God's glory. We've found the joys of service far outweigh the threat.

— Celeste S. McFarland with Kenneth Lane, aftercare coordinator, Rockbridge County Mental Health Clinic, Lexington, Virginia

Resources for Help with Deinstitutionalized People

FRIENDSHIP
Education Department of the Christian Reformed Church
2850 Kalamazoo Avenue, S.E.
Grand Rapids, MI 49560
*A Bible class series for mentally impaired children and adults.
A promotional film is available.*

Shepherd's Inc.
Box 11   Union Grove, WI 53182
A Christian residential home for the mentally handicapped that makes its material available for a small fee.

Handi-Vangelism Bible Club Movement, Inc.
237 Fairfield Ave.   Upper Darby, PA 19082
Offers training and programs to churches working with physically handicapped or mentally limited children.

Association for Retarded Citizens
2501 Avenue J   Arlington, TX 76011
ARC has a six-page bibliography on religion and religious education. They also make available booklets for those who counsel families of mentally retarded people and lead the congregation in serving the mentally retarded and their families.

Books:

77 Dynamic Ideas for the Christian Education of the Handicapped, by James Pierson (Standard)

How to Teach the Mentally Retarded, by Gloria Hawley (Victor)

Treating the Long-term Mentally Ill, by H. Richard Lamb (Jossey-Bass)

WORLD MISSIONS

Half a Letter's Better Than No Letter at All

Every pastor and missions committee would love to get the congregation writing to missionaries. Too often missionary report letters go unanswered and even unread by the supporters to whom they're addressed.

At Bethel Baptist Church in Denver, Pastor Paul Miller has decided that even a short P.S. from his members is worth cultivating. He writes a monthly mimeographed letter of church news and encouragements to the 30 missionaries the church supports. But he doesn't mail the letters; he takes them instead to a Sunday or midweek service, where ushers hand them out to volunteers.

"I ask people to jot a note on the bottom — personal news, a verse of Scripture, anything they'd like to add — and then to mail the letter themselves. Some even enclose bulletins or interesting newspaper clippings that the missionary might enjoy."

In this way, 30 different individuals or families get involved in direct communication with a missionary every month. "We've done this for more than seven years now," says Miller, "with close to 25 percent of the congregation participating at one time or another. One missionary told us that whenever she sees mail from our church, she stops immediately to read it because it's like a quick trip home. Meanwhile, our people appreciate this contact and have been delighted when missionaries have taken time to answer their notes personally in return."

Reported by Ruth Richert Jones

Letters to Missionaries: A Possible Dream

Most church members write to their favorite missionary about as often as their favorite aunt. In both cases, good intentions fall short.

A little organizing, however, ups the frequency significantly. Consider West Chicago Bible Church in Illinois, where a "22 Club" of committed letter writers has gotten mail off to the church's missionary roster on a monthly basis.

"We made an alphabetical list of the 22 missionary couples and individuals we support," says Pastor Howard Westlund, "and then asked for a matching number of people from the congregation who would commit themselves to write one letter a month. Each month they move one notch down on the list, so that each month they're writing to a new address, and the missionary is constantly hearing from new people."

How many members actually follow through?

"Occasionally we'll get 'confessions' about falling behind," says the pastor, "but my guess is that the system is working at least 75 percent of the time. I can tell by a couple of ways: (1) Missionaries have said or written to me: 'Suddenly I'm getting correspondence from a number of your people. What's happening?' Also, (2) members share with me the return letters they get from missionaries."

Every time the missionary roster needs updating, of course, the new sheet reminds 22 Club members of their responsibility. "People have settled into a routine now," says Westlund. "Whenever they turn the calendar for a new month, they almost automatically get out an aerogram.

"Along the way, we've done some educating about what to write," he adds. "Missionaries don't need preachments and Bible verses so much as news about our ordinary lives, what's been happening at the church, and so forth. It's just like writing to a friend."

MISSIONARY MAIL THAT MINISTERS

by Richard Lewis, missionary, Kitale, Kenya

To a missionary, mail is one of life's treasures. If you were ever in the military and remember standing in the rain for mail call, you know what a letter from home can mean. It's the same with missionaries. Mail can minister — if it's thoughtfully sent. In the seven years our family has been in Kenya, some things have passed through our mailbox that meant much to us.

Reading material: What magazines do you read? Would a missionary enjoy those magazines also? From time to time a fellow in the States air-mails me the latest issue of *Sports Illustrated*. Because air-mail postage is so expensive, he can't do it often, but it's a nice gesture when he does. It makes us feel like someone cares.

How about comic books for the kids, *Good Housekeeping* for the wife? Do you enjoy a subscription to *Leadership*? Do you think a missionary would? Would a missionary's wife enjoy a subscription to *Today's Christian Woman* or *Partnership*? Would the kids enjoy receiving *Campus Life*? What are their hobbies? Maybe they would like *Mechanix Illustrated, Computer Digest,* or *Creative Crafts.*

Recently a pastor sent me a book. He wrote, "I enjoyed this book; it was a blessing to my life. I thought I'd share it with you." What thoughtfulness!

Cassettes: I had been in a mud hut for a week teaching national pastors. One morning, discouraged and a little lonely, I turned on a music tape I had just received from a pastor friend. The first song was "Someone Is Praying for You," by

Praise. I can't begin to describe what that meant to me that morning.

What type of music do you enjoy? Do you think a missionary might enjoy the same? Perhaps they like classics, show music, country and western, or pop. Recently a church surprised my daughter with her own cassette recorder and some tapes.

Several pastors send a copy of their church services on tape. I have also received teaching tapes on leadership principles, finances, and motivational material. These are helpful to keep a missionary from going dry.

One year someone sent me the World Series on cassette, commercials included. As I drove my truck in the desert, I listened to Vin Scully's play-by-play. It made a four-hour journey in 100-degree heat almost enjoyable.

Video: Sitting in his home in Odessa, Texas, watching a movie on video, Rev. Jerry Thorpe turned to me and asked, "Lewis, if our church bought you a video machine, could you use it?"

"We sure could!" I answered.

Video players are difficult to get into some countries, but I don't know of a better morale booster. My family enjoys worshiping the Lord in English. After being in African churches, preaching in Swahili, it's nice to watch a video-taped American worship service. Even Bible teaching courses are available on video.

Practicality aside, my wife is a movie buff, my kids are cartoon buffs, and old Dad is a news and sports buff.

I realize some people feel old movies and cartoons don't have anything to do with the Lord's work, but if isolation is harmful to missionaries' morale, perhaps a little Americana might be of some practical use. We won't know till we get to heaven, but perhaps Paul would have enjoyed the Olympics, and Livingstone would have enjoyed a little cricket if they had been able to watch it via video.

Packages: The Women's Missionary Society of Central Baptist Church in Tyler, Texas, are pros when it comes to sending packages to missionaries.

At their meetings they bring empty milk cartons and pack them with little items not available in many parts of the world. We have received such precious American products as KoolAid, cake mixes, chocolate chips, coconut, balloons, artificial sweetener, and pocket calendars. That may not sound very exciting to you, but when you're 10,000 miles from the land of plenty, those are neat items to receive.

They aren't expensive; the value of the contents never exceeds five dollars. They send the packages surface mail, so postage is less than two dollars.

Recently we received a box from another church. They had no idea what was available here or what we could really use, so their box was a hodgepodge of — well, junk! Soap, toothpaste, used pencils, combs, and used yarn. As much as we appreciated the thought, it looked as though they had cleaned out the closet.

The key is knowing what missionaries like to receive. Write and ask what suggestions they have.

Clothes: In a Third World country like ours, many people still wear very little clothing. We work among two backward tribes. Several churches in America regularly send us used clothing for our Christians, which is well received by the Africans. If you pack well and use surface mail, you can provide clothes for thirty naked kids for about twenty-two dollars. Our men especially like to receive trousers; the women enjoy dresses and skirts.

These are just some things we have received. I would encourage churches getting involved in this minsitry to correspond with the missionary first. In some countries, customs regulations are very strict. Needs are also different. Some missionaries might not want chocolate chips but have a need for soap and used pencils.

Not everyone can go to a mission field. But if you believe in world evangelism and want to do something more personal than a mission offering, the mailbag ministry is a way to "go into all the world."

Hello, Bangkok

After sending some homegrown church families overseas as missionaries, the elders at Damascus Community Church in Boring, Oregon, wanted better communication than just monthly prayer letters. How about a phone call during the Sunday evening service?

Though it sounds outlandish, the idea has proven entirely practical. It took a bit of wiring between the telephone mouthpiece and the sound system mixer board in order to let the congregation hear both sides of the conversation. The moderator asks questions from cards submitted in advance by the audience, and the missionary responds. On several occasions, the people have even sung "Happy Birthday" to the family listening on the other end.

Initially, times were prearranged by letter two months early. Now the date of the next call is set at the end of the phone call itself.

How expensive is it? A call to the Bob Watt family in Thailand cost $42.14 for 25 minutes. Calls to closer countries such as Mexico and Austria have run less. At Damascus, the investment is viewed as worthwhile.

As one church member commented, "We tend to forget about people unless we talk to them one in a while. The phone call reminds us of what they were like when they lived here. Knowing that what we're hearing is happening right now helps us relate to the lives and experiences of our missionaries."

And on the other side of the world, missionaries are encouraged as they struggle with language study, adapting to a strange culture, or just plain homesickness.
Reported by Deborah Dunn

The Conference That Refreshes

Church missions conferences: a series of marathon meetings where missionaries talk, the congregation listens, and all go home more exhausted than they came. At least that's the stereotype.

Not in Ahwahnee, California. Pastor Glenn Davidson thinks a missions conference should be a refueling stop for missionaries. Three weekends a year, Ahwahnee Chapel offers a relaxed "Let us minister to you" experience.

"But in the process," says Davidson, "our people learn more about missions than they would sitting in meetings."

On Friday evening, with displays in place, all the participants are introduced. Two missionaries give brief slide presentations of their work. But the main focus of the evening is the food and fellowship that follows. That night missionary guests stay in homes of church members.

"When we first started these conferences, people were reluctant to open their homes," says Davidson. "But now they're standing in line, especially parents. They want their children to get to know a missionary."

Saturday morning breakfast at the church is for missionaries only, who swap stories and ideas. Then, after a devotional by the pastor, missionaries and church members share prayer requests, divide into pairs, and pray for one another. A list of the missionaries' prayer needs is printed for distribution on Sunday morning.

Saturday afternoon is free time, with members offering to take missionaries to nearby Yosemite National Park or allowing them to relax at home.

Saturday supper is shared by missionaries, deacons, and their families. Two more missionaries share a few slides, and a guest speaker gives a word of encouragement to both missionaries and members.

On Sunday, missionaries are regular worshipers, not special speakers. They may speak in a Sunday school class if they wish, and two are asked for short presentations Sunday night. But again, the focus is on personal conversations, not mass meetings.

"This is totally different," a missionary from Spain told Davidson. "We're not just giving out; we're being fed."

"Our people have been enthusiastic about this approach," says the pastor. "They've made warm friendships with missionaries. No one goes home exhausted. And we've all been spiritually fed and touched by the needs throughout the world."

Reported by Barbara King

A Conference with "Real People"

Watching slides of Nigeria is one thing. Talking to a real-live Nigerian in your living room is something else.

That's why for the past three Novembers, First Presbyterian Church in Deerfield, Illinois, has spiced its mission conferences with foreign students. After getting names from nearby Christian colleges and seminaries, "we send personalized invitations to come and be our guests in our homes for the weekend," says Pastor Bernard F. Didier.

Members gladly welcome the internationals, finding out about their countries and also discussing the presentations at church by the conference's career missionary speakers.

Side benefits include:

● Students with musical talents or slide of their countries are scheduled into the program.

- Students are given a few minutes at the two Sunday morning services to share their plans as well as prayer concerns for their countries.
- Students get to interact with each other. "The interplay among the participants," says Didier, "is as important as any one feature."

Bonds of friendship are established that often result in the students being invited back to the church.
Reported by Lawson Lau

Raise Donors, Not Dollars

When it comes to raising money for world missions, Robert Schmidgall concentrates as much on the number of people making faith promises as the number of dollars promised. That's one reason why his church, Calvary Temple in Naperville, Illinois, consistently leads the denomination (Assemblies of God) in missions giving.

"1 Corinthians 16 talks about 'every one of you' getting involved in giving, and missions is a good area to practice that. If 1,000 people give $20 a month, that's twice as good as 100 people giving $100 a month," he says. "And it also gives the congregation a feel for what we can do *together*."

The church holds two week-long missions conferences a year, in May and November. On the final Sunday morning, when faith promises are solicited for the next six months, ushers make sure every individual present receives a card. Then, when totals are announced, the number of givers gets equal time with the amount of money raised.

"I don't apologize for asking boldy when it comes to world missions," says the pastor. "Actually, it's the only time of year we make a strong push. Even the young are challenged to make their own faith promises. We send our missionary guests to the teen classes and down as far as the junior department, and many of the 'students fill out cards. Below the fourth grade, we ask parents to talk with their children about what they might do on their own apart from Mom and Dad."

The result: approximately two-thirds of the Sunday morning attenders (all ages) make faith promises to the missions fund. Fulfillment of those promises runs 90 percent. Total giving to world missions in 1981: $242.68 per capita.

A Mini Shopping Spree

Unlike Old Mother Hubbard's cupboard, the missionary shelves at Union Grove Baptist Church in Wisconsin are well stocked for furlough "shopping sprees."

Items donated by church members are assigned a point value. Stationery, books, nylons, socks, perfume, razors, shampoo, and shaving cream are 1 point each. Household items such as sheets, pillow cases, towels, bowls, and sets of glasses range from 2 to 4 points each. Children's toys, games, and puzzles vary from 1 to 3 points.

Each member of a visiting family is given 5 points of purchasing power.

"What an answer to prayer!" said Libby Basler, missionary on furlough from South America. "Some of the things we needed to set up housekeeping here were provided through the cupboard."

The children especially enjoy picking out what they want.

To keep the cupboard from going bare, the ladies' mission society designates one meeting a year for women to bring something for the cupboard. Each member also donates one item on her birthday.

Sunday school classes and youth clubs also purchase items for the cupboard.

Reported by Teresa Johnson

MISSIONS: OVERCOMING THE HO-HUM

by Richard Lewis, missionary, Kitale, Kenya

The trouble with missions in the average church is that it's a little like National Blueberry Week — nobody's opposed to it, but not too many are fired up about it, either. I shouldn't talk; during my five years as an independent Baptist pastor, missions was just another program at my church, too. We were concerned about those who hadn't heard the gospel, but the annual missions conference did not exactly generate wild enthusiasm. Forty percent participation from the members was about the best we could hope for.

Now I have been a missionary for seven years. I have spoken in almost 300 American churches, presenting my field. I've seen the best and worst of attitudes toward missions. What I've learned most is that overseas evangelism does not have to be boring.

Here are three things that dampen inspiration, followed by five that ignite it.

Bad Ideas for Missions Promotion

1. *Sprinkle out the exposure.* As a pastor, I used to have a missionary speaker an average of once every six weeks. My philosophy was, keep missions before the people, and the program will be a success. What I failed to understand was that for something to be special, it must not become overly familiar. By the time our conference rolled around, our people had seen ten missions presentations. The special element was gone.

A pastor in Illinois has only one special series a year — the missions conference. He schedules missionaries and other speakers years in advance. For 51 weeks the church is geared for that one week in November. No wonder the bulding is filled to capacity every night.

2. *Blend missions with other emphases.* As a missionary, I have been "stuck in" with many programs that had nothing to do with missions. I have shown my slides at revival meetings and Vacation Bible Schools. In both cases I was just a filler, entertainment. Missions was a side attraction, not a ministry of special importance.

3. *Use missionaries to raise other church funds.* I was invited once to speak at a stewardship conference. Each night I presented Kenya and the world's need for Christ. It wasn't until the Saturday night banquet that I saw the proposed church budget. For church operation, $100,000; building projects, $80,000; missions, $25,000 (of which $10,000 was for their bus ministry).

Using a missionary may be a quick fix for financial problems in a church, but it cannot continue year after year to bail out poor financial management.

Good Ideas for Missions Promotion

1. *Involve the young.* A church in New Mexico assigns each Sunday school department a particular mission field. Each night of the conference, one department presents a short program on a field.

The junior department was assigned the field of Kenya. Before my presentation that night, the kids paraded into the church in traditional African dress. Using newsletters I had sent the past four years as their source, they put on a play about the life of a missionary in Kenya. After the service, we went to their classrooms, where they has recreated an African village. We were served refreshments from their grass huts.

All this accomplished two things: (1) the kids learned a

great deal about a missionary and his field; (2) parents attended the meeting, if for no other reason than to see their children's program.

2. *Use food.* There's no refuting the fact that people attend functions with food!

A Springdale, Arkansas, church puts a great deal of effort into its international supper on Saturday night of the conference. Months in advance they write missionary wives for recipes that are unique to their fields. They divide the gymnasium into countries and decorate accordingly.

After supper comes the missions challenge by a good speaker.

3. *Concentrate the exposure.* One mistake I made as a pastor was not allowing people to get to know missionaries well enough. Whenever we had a conference, I would schedule a different missionary each night to put variety into the meetings — Latin America, the Far East, Africa, and Europe all in a week. The missionaries were just passing strangers in the night. Within a short time, the people forgot them all.

My wife and I were invited to a three-day conference in Tyler, Texas. The first night was for women only, supper at the church. My wife showed slides — not of the work, but of our lifestyle in Kenya: our house, our children, their school, the town where we live, our "supermarket" (the butchery and vegetable market). Afterward she fielded questions from the women. The following night it was my turn with the men. Using basically the same format, I was able to share things I would have to skip in a formal service.

The low-key approach may not suit every church, but it was very successful for them. On Sunday morning, their mission commitment for the coming year was $100,000.

4. *Get missionaries and members in one-to-one contact.* As much as I personally like to stay in a motel, some interchanges are possible only in living rooms. People want to know what makes a person serve Christ 10,000 miles from home. Many nights I've been kept up late by families quizzing me

about Kenya, and the personal contact has always been worth the inconvenience.

5. *Give more than money.* A membership that does something personalized for a missionary is prone to be more interested.

A church in Oxnard, California, asked my wife and me to send a list of our needs — not major things, but items costing under $100. When they received the list, they put it on a blackboard in the foyer of the church. Members would then choose items and erase them from the blackboard.

The last night of the conference was called "Christmas in September." The people brought wrapped gifts and placed them underneath a tree on the platform. Sandy and I were overwhelmed as we unwrapped these gifts, and the people were excited to meet particular needs.

Missions *can* be exciting — if it is well planned and made special. Christians in America can be moved not only to give, to pray, and to understand — but to enjoy it.

THE CHURCH YEAR

The New Year's Sermon that Echoed

"How do we avoid having just another sermon that's forgotten before dinner is over?"

That was the question raised by the worship committee at Calvary Memorial Church in Oak Park, Illinois, after learning that Pastor Donald Gerig intended to kick off the new year with a message on spiritual growth.

The eventual solution: a blank piece of paper and an envelope inside every bulletin. "At the close of the sermon, I gave the people a few minutes to write a letter to themselves," Gerig says, "outlining goals for their own growth. Then they sealed the envelope, addressed it, and turned it in. We promised we'd mail it back to them six months later as a check-up."

Some stayed in the pews that morning, busily writing, while others turned theirs in as much as a month later. Altogether about 40 percent of the audience responded.

That June, the letters went out to remind people of their aspirations. "It was a positive growth experience for many," Gerig remembers. "Quite a few expressed appreciation for the reminder." It was certainly one message that outlasted the afternoon football game.

A Cross to Survey

No one misses the beginning of Lent at the Zion and Salem Presbyterian churches near Alton, Illinois. The two yoked congregations open the season's first Sunday with a dramatic visual symbol: the elders at each church enter the sanctuary carrying a rugged eight-foot cross and place it at the front.

"Then on the successive Sundays, different members of the congregations add elements of the crucifixion while appropriate passages of Scripture are read," explains John Seibert, pastor of both churches.

- *Second Sunday of Lent:* a whip, draped over the crossbeam
  - *Third Sunday:* a crown of thorns
  - *Fourth Sunday:* a purple robe
  - *Fifth Sunday:* large spikes (hammered into predrilled holes)

"Zion's cross is made of sawmill slabs, lashed together with rope," Seibert adds. "Salem's is made of barn timbers. We don't try to beautify these things. Our children are in the worship services along with the adults, and we want everyone to realize what actually happened in Christ's sacrifice."

The crosses stay in place through Maundy Thursday and Good Friday, but are gone on Easter morning.

Forsythias for the King

When Jesus made his triumphal entry into Jerusalem, the crowds cheered and laid palm branches at his feet. Since palm trees are rare in Salem, Oregon, the people at Redeemer Lutheran Church used something more fragrant for their march — spring flowers.

"For Palm Sunday, we asked each person to bring at least one flower to place on the altar during the service," says Pastor James Schackel, who has since moved to a church in Montrose, Colorado. "We also had several dozen on hand at church for visitors and those who forgot."

Then, following the Gospel lesson, the congregation rose to sing "Ride On, Ride On in Majesty" and other Palm Sunday hymns. Meanwhile, row by row, the people came forward to offer their forsythias, tulips, daffodils, and camellias.

One woman was stationed at the altar to arrange

the flowers for maximum visibility throughout the sanctuary.

"Both children and adults enjoyed being a part of the Palm Sunday parade. At the end, the cumulative effect of the pile of flowers was impressive and inspirational," says Schackel. "We experienced something of what the people must have felt when Jesus came into Jerusalem."

A Night for Tradition

Almost every Christian has wondered, "What was it really like at the Last Supper?" To have sat at the table with the Twelve, to listen to Jesus' words, to feel the tension and pathos in the air . . . one can only imagine.

The people of First Church of the Nazarene in Frederick, Maryland, have had a replay of sorts the past few years through a Passover Seder service on Maundy Thursday. A Seder is the Jewish commemoration of the Exodus that was repeated in the Upper Room that fateful night. "I've wanted to help people feel and appreciate the events leading up to the cross," says Pastor Robert A. Walter. "We try to identify with our Lord as he prepared to be crucified for our sins."

The service includes the reading of the psalms that are traditionally sung in a Seder, the use of unleavened bread and the cup, and even the distributing of bitter herbs among the congregation — all to show how Jesus used the Old Testament celebration to introduce the Lord's Supper. The 1982 service had a new feature: the associate pastor chanted the psalms cantor-style.

Pastor Walter wrote his own script for the service after taking a course in Jewish culture. Among his sources: *The Passover Anthology,* edited by Philip Goodman (Philadelphia: Jewish Publication Society of America, 1961) and *Eerdman's Handbook to the Bible.* Other churches have invited outside guests (Hebrew

Christians, or those who work in Jewish evangelism) to come in and lead a Seder for them.

In the Frederick church, the Thursday night Seder replaces the traditional Good Friday afternoon service, although a community-wide service is available to those who want both.

Crucified for Me

The meaning of Good Friday sometimes gets lost as Christians look forward to Easter two days later.

But at Zion Lutheran Church in Moberly, Missouri, one Good Friday service made a lasting impact.

"Some people in our congregation had trouble applying the crucifixion to their lives," says Pastor G. R. Hoffstetter. "To help bring it home, we made a cross of rough cedar and placed it in front of the altar."

The six-foot cross, made of four-by-fours mounted on a circular wooden base, was more than the visual center of the service.

"Before the Scripture lesson was read," the pastor explains, "I invited people to write their names on the sheets of paper we'd distributed that said, 'Jesus Christ died for _____.' "

When the reading was done, 50 persons — almost everyone there — came up one by one to nail their names to the cross. The church was silent except for the pounding of the hammer. Acolytes helped stabilize the cross and assisted those who had trouble wielding the hammer.

Hoffstetter reports the response was excellent. Like another crucifixion long ago, this one helped make one Friday especially good.

The "He Arose" Garden

For some people Easter means chocolate rabbits, camouflaged eggs, and a corsage. But for Dorothy Heinmiller and the people at Hollywood Lutheran Church in California, it takes on a fresh meaning thanks to rocks, dirt, plants . . . and Dorothy's painstaking creativity.

Each year, several weeks before Easter, Dorothy creates a four-by-eight foot Easter rock garden on the floor of the narthex. On one side is a hill with three crosses. On the center cross is tacked an inscription in Latin, Greek, and Aramaic: "Jesus, King of the Jews." Across the way is a tomb — made of three flat rocks covered by an abalone shell and moss. A flat, round rock — perhaps four inches in diameter — guards the entrance.

Around the rest of the garden, rocks and flowers — African violets, begonias, ornamental palms, caladiums — are artistically arranged.

A layer of plastic trash bags, topped by a layer of newspaper, topped by another layer of plastic, prevents moisture from seeping into the carpet. Bricks around the border keep the potting soil from spilling out. It takes Dorothy two days to assemble the visual reminder of Christ's death and resurrection.

On Good Friday, the stone is rolled in front of the tomb. On Easter, the stone is rolled away, and inside on a rock shelf are empty grave clothes (strips of white cloth). A small light illumines the inside of the tomb.

"Dorothy's project blesses and blesses each year," says her pastor, Harry Durkee. "What a sight to see the eyes of the children widen as the Easter story is told as they stand by the Easter garden."
Reported by Mildred Tengbom

Prayer for the Plowing

The quiet hopes — and fears — of farmers get special attention each spring at Community Christian Church, Barnes City, Iowa. As soon as the ground thaws and field work begins in earnest, Pastor Douglas Smiley has a special time of prayer at the close of a Sunday morning service for all who will work in agriculture over the coming months.

"We do this for two reasons," he explains. "First, we recognize that farming is a dangerous occupation, and we want to ask God's protection for those working with powerful machinery. Second, the church through the centuries has always asked God to bless the seeds and the fields, to send rain at the right times for the provision of food."

Approximately half the Barnes City church are either husbands and wives who farm or young people who will work on farms throughout the summer. Smiley invites them forward to the altar area at the end of his sermon, has them join hands, and then calls the rest of the congregation to surround the group as a sign of their concern. Together they pray for stamina, for wisdom in managing funds, for protection from danger, and for good crops.

"We've done this for five years or so," says the pastor, "and I always hear words of appreciation — not only from the women, who sometimes worry about their husbands' safety, but from the men as well. They feel it's important for the church to do this, to agree together before the Lord as they begin their busy season."

Reviving Revivals

At one time, revival meetings were a creative innovation. The weeklong series of evening meetings would attract unbelievers, marginal churchgoers, and committed

Christians needing a spiritual boost. Churches are still adding creative touches to the old and cherished tradition. Here are two:

The elderly woman from West 87th Street in New York City was pleased. She had been able to attend the meetings at her church, First Baptist, thanks to a thoughtful innovation — services at 11 A.M. in addition to the evening meetings.

"Many of us older people are afraid to go out at night," she says. "Our eyes aren't as good as they once were, and often weather is harsher after dark."

Older folks weren't the only ones to benefit. In the 24-hour-a-day pulse of today's cities, thousand of people work night shifts.

"Also attending were a surprising number of young wives and mothers," says Tim Means, the pastor who decided to experiment with the morning revival. "In many homes, women must be at home in the evenings. Plus, lots of times in one-parent families, it's easier to come while the children are in school."

Attendance at the morning sessions wasn't as great as at night, but "enough people attended to make it more than worth the effort," says Means.

"Day people need God, too."
Reported by Mary Louise Kitsen

Recently the Modoc, Indiana, Church of the Nazarene observed the Year of the Layman. What better way than to have laypeople speak during the week of revival?

"Our nightly speakers were men and women from other Nazarene churches in the area," says Pastor Bill Evans. "I'd met several key laypersons from other churches in our district meetings and knew they had something to say. So our board asked them to speak on the layman's responsibility in the local church, but they were free to choose their own topics."

An insurance agent gave a devotional meditation from Psalm 91.

The wife of a funeral director spoke on the marks of a Christian woman.

A veterinarian who serves as superintendent of his church school spoke on the importance of Sunday school.

The Tuesday through Sunday meetings "reaffirmed the importance of the laity in our church," says Evans. "It was living proof that the life of holiness can be lived in the marketplace.

"But maybe the best thing we realized was that we are not alone — other people are serving their churches and God's kingdom in situations very similar to ours. That was encouraging."

Summer Film Fair

Shortly after arriving at Zion United Methodist Church in Juda, Wisconsin (pop. 300), Ray Steger took a long look at the facilities. Eventually his eyes came to the parking lot.

"It was only used once a week to its fullest," says Steger. "So I tried to think of ways that vacant space could be used for ministry."

Suddenly came a creative flash. *Why not an outdoor movie for Juda?*

"The only outdoor theater, 12 miles away, shows R- and X-rated pictures," says Steger. "I figured we could provide a better way for families to spend a summer evening."

So Steger announced that the church would show three films during the summer: *In God We Trust, A Boy Named David,* and *Touch of the Master's Hand.*

Leaflets were inserted in the church bulletin. Posters were displayed in grocery store windows in Juda and in nearby Monroe and Brodhead. The parking lot was partially roped off, and volunteers set up church chairs. Some brought lawn chairs from home.

Admission was free, though an offering plate set on

a chair helped defray the cost. People were encouraged to bring their own popcorn and drinks. Religious music played 15 minutes before the show began.

"The response was gratifying," says Steger. "We'll be doing it again this summer, with a better screen mounted from brackets in the roof overhang. People have already been asking what we plan to show and whether we'll show more than three."

To the Barracks with Love

Independence Day, 1982, came on a Sunday, and Prince of Peace Lutheran Church in Woodridge, Illinois, paid special attention to five people who weren't there — members of the church on military duty.

Five sheets of church stationery were taped to a table in the narthex, and worshipers were invited to stop and jot a sentence or two. All ages, from children to adults, ended up filling both sides of the sheet with cheery greetings and news. The pastor, Albert Weidlich, added a note to each and then dropped them in the mail.

"One man who was discharged two months later made a special trip to see me," says Weidlich, "to say how good it felt to be remembered by his home church."

The liturgy that Sunday also included a special prayer for chaplains and others in the armed forces.

(Extra hint from this pastor: When providing pens for writing at such a table, put them out *without caps.* That way, people don't walk off with them!)

Liberty Month

The July celebration of American freedom is tempered in at least one church by a concern for fellow believers who have little to celebrate.

"Each Sunday of July," says Lloyd Jacobsen, pastor of Bethel Temple in St. Paul, Minnesota, "we focus on a different area of the world where Christians are presently suffering persecution." The emphasis happens in three ways:

• A large bulletin board in the narthex that highlights the geography — not only of the Soviet Union and China but areas such as the Middle East and Central America. Photos, news clippings, and statistics help tell the sobering stories.

• A special intercession time in the morning service each week; also, a bulletin insert highlighting that week's region.

• Encouragement for church members to continue their intercession throughout the week during personal and family devotions.

"Liberty Month has enlarged our vision and helped us think more in terms of the body of Christ worldwide," says Jacobsen. "The Scriptures admonish us to pray for brothers and sisters undergoing trials, and we think this is a good thing to do in the context of July 4."

In Praise of Labor Day

What does working have to do with worshiping? A lot, says W. Philip Coe, minister at First Christian Church in Sac City, Iowa. To highlight labor in a Christian context, he has begun constructing sermons for Labor Day weekends that incorporate slide shows of his parishioners on the job.

"I try to lift up the dignity of work — all kinds," says Coe, "and I weave in the comments of my people on why they're proud of what they do, what they enjoy about it. Some mention the contact with people, others the pleasure of being outdoors, and so forth. Meanwhile, on the screen appears one of our men on his tractor, or a beautician, or a chiropractor in his office, a fellow on his milk truck route, a farm housewife, a nurse in a hospital corridor, a carpenter."

The presentation, which usually takes 20 minutes or so, includes biblical texts about work along with the parishioners' comments. "After all, this is where their lives are invested, where they work out their faith," says Coe.

Having recently acquired his own camera, the pastor intends to shoot slides throughout the year from now on in order to include other seasons besides summer. "Naturally, the people are very responsive to these Sundays," he says. "They appreciate the personal touch."

A Full-Blown Conference for Less

Can a small-town church of fewer than 100 afford a Family Life Emphasis weekend with four different specialists?

Probably not . . . unless it economizes by joining in a round-robin arrangement with other churches nearby. That's what eight Baptist congregations in northwest Texas, ranging from 65 to 450, did. Each was able to provide a four-session conference (Friday night, Saturday night, twice on Sunday).

"The larger churches chipped in $350 and the smaller ones $250," says Travis Hart, pastor of First Baptist in Olton. "Plus, our association made a donation and also printed our publicity materials."

The savings came not so much in honoraria as in travel expenses, which were spread over multiple engagements. Two of the speakers were directors of counseling programs, one a professional writer, and the other a Wayland Baptist University professor.

"We held the seminars on two different weekends," Hart explains, "four churches on one weekend and four on the other. So each speaker had to prepare only one presentation — his specialty — and then give it in eight different locations. Each church hosted one faculty member, providing lodging, meals, and transportation during the weekend."

A post-conference evaluation by the eight pastors was positive for two reasons: the costs had been curtailed, and the churches had received better, more wide-ranging help for families than any of them could have managed with a single speaker.

First, a Feast

The warmth of Thanksgiving becomes literal at Ivanhoe Reformed Church, Riverdale, Illinois, as soon as a "Feast in the Woods" committee member lights the early-morning fire in the forest preserve shelter house. By 7:30, the first families will be arriving, bringing their coffee cake, doughnuts, or special bread to go with the already prepared coffee, juice, and hot chocolate.

"It doesn't matter whether the weather is good or not," says Pastor Thomas Bartha. "There's a roof over our heads and a fireplace at each end of the shelter. Adults and children alike have a great time eating, talking, and staying warm around the fires. Some even bring along Frisbees."

More than two-thirds of this congregation of 100 came to last year's feast, which included scrambled eggs and sausage.

Then the group drives directly to the church (15 minutes away) for the 10:00 A.M. Thanksgiving service. The outdoor attire — plaid flannel shirts, jeans, even boots — are welcome this once as the congregation enjoys, in Bartha's words, "an especially thankful feeling during worship together."

Thanksgetting to Thanksgive

Telling people to be thankful is a bit like requesting a kiss. If you have to ask for it, it usually isn't worth getting. Gratitude — and affection — lose something unless they're freely given.

But thanks to a bit of creativity and whimsy, Pastor Dean Ryder of First Baptist Church in Newfane, New York, was able to encourage people to be thankful — freely, voluntarily, and spontaneously.

The method was a reverse offering. One Sunday the offering plates were loaded with envelopes, and as the ushers passed them, everyone was told to take one. Each envelope contained a dollar bill and an index card. The instructions:

1. Decide on an individual, not part of your family, for whom you are especially thankful.

2. Express your thankfulness to God for this person.

3. Do something for this individual with the dollar and let him or her know of your thankfulness.

4. Report on what you did, using the index card in the envelope.

"We passed out $80 that morning," says Ryder. "And we collected the cards over the next few weeks. More than 85 percent of those taking an envelope turned in the card telling what they had done. I compiled the responses and read them the Sunday morning before Thanksgiving. It was a real celebration of joy."

One lady, a wood carver, spent the dollar on a block of wood and crafted a miniature dog as a gift.

Someone else made a fruit basket and delivered it, while others gave plants, cards, or carnations.

"Someone gave one woman four pieces of candy with the instructions to share three of them with people *she* was thankful for," says Ryder. "And personally I received a crock of cookies, two cards, and a sack of peanuts. I was a little embarrassed, because I hadn't done this project with the intention of being on the receiving end. But I guess we must learn to be good receivers as well as good givers."

Don't Save the Best Till Last

Abraham Lincoln managed to say something memorable at the end of a long dedication ceremony at Gettysburg — but he may have been a rare exception. Less gifted speakers at such occasions have trouble keeping their audiences awake, especially in the late afternoon.

Hence a bit of common sense: when planning a church dedication or other ceremony with many elements, put the speaker on *early*. That's what Arthur Fretheim did at the dedication of the Evangelical Covenant Church in Naperville, Illinois. The service began at 3 P.M., and after no more than a call to worship, a hymn, invocation, Scripture, prayer, and a choral anthem, the denominational president was introduced to preach while the large crowd was still alert.

Following the sermon came the day's expected formalities: comments by the building committee chairman, architect, and general contractor; transfer of the keys; presentation of grants; the litany of dedication; the special offering; and closing music. It was a full afternoon, but the speaker's challenge received the attention it deserved.

"To me, a dedication service is not just a tradition or protocol," says Fretheim, a career church planter. "This is my sixth congregation to build a building, and I've organized the last three dedications this way.

"The sermon is more than just a 10-minute necessity in the program; it's a chance to call for real commitment to the work and life of the church. That's why it deserves good placement."

Home-Grown Devotions

The Otterbein United Methodist Church in Harrisonburg, Virginia, doesn't buy devotional guides for Advent. It writes them.

Members of the congregation prepare an inspirational message for each day of the season. Louis E. Carson, pastor, says, "The idea of the 'in-house' devotional guide has proved to be one of the most creative things we have done at Otterbein in a long time. Members have responded well in submitting devotionals. When the guide is completed, it's received and used with enthusiasm."

A section for children includes stories, poems, and word games related to the season. Members who have artistic talent do the illustrations. The worship committee and one of the women's groups type and prepare the guide for printing. Afterward, they also assemble the booklets for distribution the first Sunday of Advent.

Each family is encouraged to use the booklet for daily devotions. The ministers and laypeople take it to shut-ins as well.

"Daily contact with others in the church through this devotional guide creates a stronger bond within the church family," says Carson. The church does a similar booklet for Lent each spring.
Reported by Wanda Baker

A Truly Free Lunch

When the women's fellowship of a church in Elk Grove Village, Illinois, planned its Christmas food giving one year, someone suggested they do two things:
- Cook the festive meals themselves.
- Have them distributed anonymously.

"We wanted to express our love for the Lord wihout receiving a lot of credit," says the pastor's wife. So the group worked through Community Services, a municipal agency. The meals were distributed to needy families with only a mention that they came from "one of the churches in the community."

The pastor sees great benefit in the anonymity. "All of the churches profited from the good will created," he says. "Furthermore, by going through Community Services, we had a chance to witness to decision makers in local government. Two of them wrote letters of appreciation.

"But the women didn't want me even to announce from the pulpit what they were doing. They honestly wanted to do all that work with no opportunity to be complimented. It was a gift of love."
Reported by Henry Jauhiainen

An Afternoon in Bethlehem

Heads tilt and eyes widen as preschoolers take the measure of a big Roman soldier. From sandaled feet to tufted helmet and tall spear, he is an awesome sight. But their fears are soon allayed by his warm smile as he directs them to the census taker's table. "Everyone must register before entering Bethlehem today," he says.

The children have come off a busy street into an ancient world re-created each December in the great hall of Gary Memorial United Methodist Church in Wheaton, Illinois. There awaits a living facsimile of Bethlehem's marketplace.

As visitors wend their way through the village "streets" (aisles), they may chat with merchants about their baskets, linen, brass, copper, wood, and pottery. They can shout at spitting geese and pet some real lambs. Food sellers offer samples of bread and cheese. Visitors observe as a learned rabbi urges a group of young men to concentrate on Hebrew law.

In the square, costumed children dance to the happy sound of a flute, and visitors are invited to join a game played by another circle of children using small stones.

Near the inn are shepherds, who talk to visitors about a bright star and angels who sang the night before. And behind the inn, in a dimly lit stable, are Mary and Joseph and an infant. Joseph and Mary talk about their long journey and show off their wiggly new baby.

It has taken months to create the sets, make costumes, and gather props for this elaborate drama. Gary Church has been offering this gift to its community for nine years, and each year it has been refined and supplemented.

Thousands of yards of fireproofed muslin and rope are used to create the various booths in the marketplace. Brass, copper, and straw utensils are collected from church members and friends. Living plants are everywhere, giving an outdoor feeling, and pens of animals baaing and braying raise the noise level. A small platform at one end of the hall becomes a synagogue. Scripts are written for all participants, from merchants to money changers to beggars.

In a single Sunday afternoon the drama is shared with as many as 2,000 people. The volume of visitors is wisely controlled, so that the hall never becomes overcrowded. Those waiting are invited to sit in the beautifully decorated sanctuary, where they join in carol singing with the church's chancel choir and handbell choirs.

Costumed ushers hand out printed programs with a diagram of the marketplace, the names of the participants, and the story of how the drama is prepared. Also printed is the scriptural story of the birth of Jesus. As visitors leave the hall, they are offered a scroll from a decorated Christmas tree. Inside is a printed Scripture portion. No admission fee is charged, but it is suggested that nonperishable food items may be donated for Christmas distribution to the needy.

Each year a banner across the street and stories in the newspaper announce the drama. Although television companies have asked to tape during the event, the church has always said no. To them, it is not a media event, but a worship experience.

Every year something happens to convince the church members that the effort is worthwhile. In 1982 a note was found tucked into the manger where the baby had lain. Written in childish cursive on an offering envelope from the sanctuary, it said simply, "I love you, Baby Jesus."
Reported by Bonnie Rice

A New Job for Santa Claus

What to do about the fat man in red?

A planning committee at Grace Presbyterian Church, Fort Myers, Florida, was struggling last year with how to turn children's attention to giving rather than receiving. It came up with a novel idea: have Santa Claus show up at the Christmas congregational dinner with an *empty* sack.

Instead of passing out gifts, he would *collect* gifts to be distributed at a county temporary-care shelter for children.

"We announced in advance the age span of the children in the home," says Pastor W. E. Lytch, "and urged our people to show the true spirit of Christmas by bringing wrapped gifts to the dinner. Obviously there was nothing in the county budget for this kind of thing, and it gave us a good opportunity to share."

The Gift Rap

Churches often send Christmas gifts to missionaries, but sometimes their college-age children are overlooked.

Not at Bethel Evangelical Free Church on Staten Island, New York.

For the past two years, a major portion of the special missionary Christmas offering has been sent to the half dozen MKs (missionary kids) attending colleges in the United States.

Each student receives a $10 gift certificate for a telephone call to Mom and Dad.

"We let them know we care," says Pastor Robert De Ritter. "The gifts help bridge the distance, and it's appreciated at both ends of the line."

For Families of All Shapes

Churches often take advantage of Christmas to focus on family togetherness: one family may light the church's Advent candles, another may read the Christmas story to the congregation, yet another may lead a service of carols. Usually the families picked include father, mother, and two children. That family structure, however, has become the exception rather than the rule.

"Our congregation includes an assortment of family arrangements," says Kenneth Gibble, pastor of Ridgeway Comunity Church of the Brethren in Harrisburg, Pennsylvania, "from single-person families to reconstructed families with children that are 'yours, mine, and ours.' We didn't want these people to feel less than legitimate by ignoring them during Advent."

As a result, Gibble makes a special effort to use families that don't fit the traditional mold. Last year, for instance, four church families took their turn lighting the Advent candles. They included:

- a reconstructed family
- a single person (a widow in her late forties)
- a married couple without children
- a divorced mother with two children

"In coming years we hope to involve other types of families — perhaps an 'empty nest' couple, a family with adopted or foster children, a family with a handicapped member, a three-generation family, or a family with an absentee parent because of work obligations," says Gibble.

Joy to Another World

While other church carolers bring Christmas cheer to friends and shut-ins, a San Francisco group sings in a far seamier setting: the city's bars.

Absurd? Not when you stop to think that "taverns are full of lonely people who can't face yet another night at home with the TV," says David Smith, associate director of a fellowship called His Way.

"We bring a guitar and start singing on the sidewalk outside," he explains. "Soon the door swings open, and several faces peek out. For a moment, they're bewildered, but soon they start grinning and invite us to come inside."

The group files into the dimly lit room and leads three or four familiar carols, loaning out song books they've brought along. Often requests begin popping up from the customers. Memories of past Christmases start to flood their minds, and tears well up here and there.

Then comes the crucial link: passing out a small wrapped gift to the bartender and each patron. Inside: a copy of the New Testament, with the phone number of His Way's 24-hour counseling line on the flyleaf.

"We've been doing this two or more nights a year since 1979," says Smith, "and the results are always just great. There's always a drunk or two who wants to buy you a drink, but you just say no thanks. Meanwhile, serious conversations spring up right on the spot, allowing us to share the Good News one-to-one with people trying to escape their hurt and loneliness. Others call us later and want to talk.

"The secret of our approach is no condemnation — just Christmas caroling and a gift. We've only been turned away once, when we had some of our kids with us, and a bartender was afraid a city ordinance might be broken by letting them inside. Others have checked first to make sure we weren't a cult trying to take up a collection.

"But more often, they want us to stay and sing all night. At one place, the bartender was hosting a private party for a group of laid-off dock workers. We not only led them in singing carols but wound up praying the Lord's Prayer together. The atmosphere was totally changed as we said good-by."

Evangelistic Christmas caroling? Well, why not?

What Child Is This?

Christmas carolers on your front lawn are always a welcome surprise, but the singers got a surprise of their own a few years ago in Vacaville, California.

The group from Church of the New Covenant made the rounds of several elderly families, brightening the air with songs and letting children present their handmade gifts. Then the bus began heading away from the residential streets toward the open country. "Finally we stopped by an old barn," says Colleen Britton, coordinator of Christian education. "Voices and flickering lanterns beckoned us to come inside.

"There in a corner we found Mary and Joseph — high school students in costume — watching over the babe in the manger. The scene seemed so real with the smell of straw on the floor and the noises of animals in the barn. It took us all back nearly 2,000 years.

"We listened with an even greater sense of awe as the Christmas story from Luke was read by candlelight."

The evening ended with a final stanza of "Silent Night," followed by hot chocolate and donuts on the cold December night in the stable.